Better Homes and
OUTDOOR STRUCTURES
D.I.Y

M U R D O C H   B O O K S®

Sydney • London • Vancouver

THE JOY OF OUTDOOR LIVING

Gardens these days are more than just places to grow plants; even the keenest of gardeners has embraced the idea of 'outdoor living'. We want our gardens to provide us with places to sit, to entertain, to have a meal when the weather suits and the mood strikes us. We want places where the children can play—and if there are people who don't enjoy a barbecue now and again, we have yet to meet them.

One result of this is that our gardens need more in the way of structures and furniture than they used to. If you only went out into the garden to admire the flowers or, more likely, to spend your time weeding and pruning so that passers-by could admire them—no wonder so many people decided they didn't like gardening!—it didn't matter much if the only place to sit was on the damp lawn or if there was little shade. But now we want to be able to sit without getting grass stains on our clothes or to set out a table (or better yet, to find one waiting) for an impromptu lunch, all in the comfort of shade in the summer and a sunny spot out of the wind in spring or autumn.

For this we need paved patios and decks, pergolas to shade them, screens to ensure their privacy and keep the wind off, and seats and tables that can stay out in the weather and don't have to be carted in and out of the house. None of these structures comes cheap if you have to call in a builder, but happily none is beyond the skill of anyone but the most incurably butter-fingered to build.

We have selected over forty projects, ranging from pergolas to small window boxes to enhance the live-ability of any garden. Adjust the proportions and decorative details to suit your own taste and the style of your house, and don't worry that structures in the garden will make it look like a builder's playground. With a year or two of growth, plants will soon put any structure, no matter how raw it looked when new, firmly in its place.

An arbour such as this can provide a sheltered place to sit and enjoy the garden. At first it may look a bit bare, but vines or climbers grown over it will eventually soften its appearance.

CONTENTS

Paving need not be formal. These stones look entirely natural.

PERGOLAS, ARBOURS

Pergola supports can be attractive features of the garden in themselves.

A well-designed pergola can be used to enhance the appearance of your house.

Summertime is the time for outdoor living, but in our hot climate it's no fun without shade. Trees will provide shade, but they take time to grow, and a tree large enough to give you a useful area of shade may be too large to fit comfortably in your garden plans. A pergola can be the answer. Clad with vines it gives the same cool shade shot with sunlight as a tree, and in much less time—plant annual vines such as morning glories or *Cobaea scandens* in spring and you'll have shade for Christmas. But you don't have to use vines—several of our structures are covered with closely spaced battens for instant shade. (If you prefer vines, just leave the battens off when building.) Shadecloth and canvas are possibilities too; it all depends on the style of your house and garden.

We usually think of pergolas as attached to the house, but they need not be—they can be free-standing, to shade a path or create a secluded spot for a seat. Just think where you need shade or an attractive feature and plan from there.

Enclose a structure with walls and a roof, and you have a shed. 'Shed' sounds cheap and awful—but we will show you how to make it as stylish as any house. Use it to house the lawnmower, the spade and the bicycles, or it could equally well serve as a studio or an office.

Don't forget that these are substantial structures that will need the approval of your local council. Check, too, that access to easements, water mains and sewers will not be blocked, and that you won't be cutting down light and air to internal rooms. If you are not an experienced builder, begin by reading the boxes 'Selecting timber' on page 35 and 'Timber conditions' on page 40. All the timber sizes in this chapter are rough sawn or nominal.

AND GARDEN SHEDS

A pergola covered with canvas or shadecloth will make a comfortable outdoor living area for hot summer days.

GARDEN SEAT ARBOUR

Only simple woodworking techniques are needed to make this comfortable and attractive arbour with seat.
Paint or varnish the finished structure to blend with your garden, or leave it to weather.

This garden seat will make a pretty focus for your garden, as well as a destination for a stroll and a place to sit while viewing the results of your gardening efforts. The openwork sides can be used as a trellis to support climbing plants.

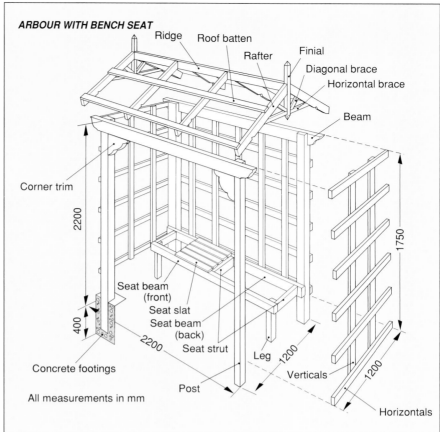

ARBOUR WITH BENCH SEAT

Ridge — Roof batten — Rafter — Finial — Diagonal brace — Horizontal brace — Beam — Corner trim — Seat beam (front) — Seat slat — Seat beam (back) — Seat strut — Leg — Verticals — Concrete footings — Post — Horizontals

2200 — 400 — 2200 — 1750 — 1200 — 1200

All measurements in mm

MATERIALS LIST

Component	Material	Length/size (mm)	Quantity
Post	100 x 100 mm treated pine	2600	4
Beam	150 x 50 mm treated pine	2400	2
Rafter	100 x 50 mm treated pine	1800	8
Ridge	100 x 50 mm treated pine	2300	1
Finial	50 x 50 mm treated pine	1200	2
Diagonal brace	38 x 38 mm treated pine	400	4
Horizontal brace	75 x 38 mm hardwood	850	2
Roof batten	75 x 25 mm treated pine	2300	4
Seat beam (front)	75 x 38 mm treated pine	2010	1
Seat beam (back)	75 x 38 mm treated pine	2200	1
Seat strut	75 x 38 mm hardwood	312	3
Leg	75 x 75 mm treated pine	420	2
Seat slat	75 x 25 mm hardwood	2100	5
Back horizontals	75 x 19 mm hardwood	2200	5
Side horizontals	75 x 19 mm hardwood	1200	12
Verticals	75 x 19 mm hardwood	1750	9

Other: Four bags pre-mixed concrete, eight 100 mm bolts with washers and nuts for frame corners, galvanised 37 mm clouts for verticals and horizontals, 75 mm bullet-head nails for roof frame, eight 100 mm coach screws for seat

BUILDING THE GARDEN SEAT ARBOUR

1 Peg out the site using the dimensions on our drawing as a guide. Dig all the holes approximately 400 mm deep, depending on the degree of site slope.

2 Make two U shapes for front and back, using the posts and two beams. Shape ends of the beams and cut out the top of the posts so the beams sit flush. Drill and bolt joints.

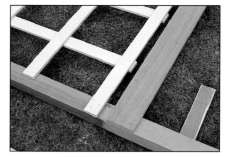

3 Nail a temporary brace 500 mm up from the bottom of the posts to keep the two frames square and add a 365 mm grid of hardwood verticals and horizontals to the back.

5 Stand posts in holes. Use a level to check they are perfectly vertical and the beams are horizontal. Prop the posts in place.

6 Make sure that the two frames are at the same height before filling the holes with concrete and leaving for forty-eight hours.

7 Make the two gables to a 30 degree pitch, cutting a half-lap joint at the intersection of finial and horizontal brace.

9 For total accuracy, stack the gables and rafters together to mark on them the position of the roof battens.

10 Now make up the two sides of the roof by nailing the battens to the two central rafters. Check diagonals for square.

11 Nail one side of the roof to the two gables, then position the ridge and lastly nail on the second side.

13 Make up panels of side verticals and horizontals and then nail them to the corner posts.

14 Make up the seat platform with its five seat slats according to the drawing.

15 Coach screw the back beam of the seat to the posts and the legs to the front of the seat.

4 Check that diagonal measurements are the same to establish that the structure is perfectly square. Nail a temporary diagonal brace across one corner.

8 Cut out birds' mouths from the rafters where they will sit on the beams. Skew nail all the joints and undercoat as you proceed.

12 You will need help to lift the roof structure into place. Set birds' mouths over each beam and skew nail rafters to beams.

16 Drill and jigsaw post trims and screw in place. Then sit back and relax.

SIMPLE ARBOUR

A simple arbour can be built in a few hours, even if you are relatively new to woodworking. Covered with a climbing rose, it will make a beautiful focal point in your garden, or use it to add interest to a gate.

1 Erect two posts (see page 17). Fix two short lengths of 150 x 50 mm timber to each post. Check to be sure these cross-beams are centred on the posts and square with them before tightening the fixing screws.

2 If desired, use a jigsaw or a router in order to shape a decorative motif at the ends of the two longer beams. Drive at least two nails through these into the ends of each cross-beam.

3 Cut 50 x 50 mm battens to length and drive one nail through each into each of the longer beams. To minimise measuring, use spacer blocks when fixing the battens.

BUILDING A PERGOLA

This basic pergola can be built in ten easy steps (see pages 12–13). Vary the plan to suit your house and garden.

The easiest way to extend your living area and provide a cool, comfortable place to sit on a hot summer day is to build a pergola. You can add a pergola to an existing deck or patio, or plan it as part of a new outdoor living area. It is important to provide adequate footings for the posts but framing need not be as strong as for a deck as pergola roofing materials are usually lightweight. The framing must, of course, be sturdy enough to withstand strong winds and avoid collapsing under the weight of leaves or, in cold areas, snow.

post bracket in it (diagram 2). If you are adding a pergola to an existing patio, position the posts just outside the patio to avoid having to break into the concrete. Dig post holes (about 230 mm in diameter and 300 mm deep is usually large enough) in the required places, put gravel in the holes for drainage and set the posts in concrete (diagram 3). For more on erecting posts see the box on page 17.

ATTACHING THE PERGOLA TO A HOUSE

A pergola is attached to the house with a ledger. To attach a ledger to a one-storey house, fix it to the wall studs below the eaves, using 100 mm masonry bolts for brick or stone walls. If your house is weatherboard, attach the ledger to the wall studs (through the board) using 75 mm coach bolts. This way the pergola will be just below roof level (see diagram 1, below).

To attach a ledger to a two-storey house, use masonry bolts or coach screws to fix it to the upper storey floor framing. To locate the joists, measure up from a window, inside and out. Make allowance for the thickness of ceiling materials (see diagram 2, below).

CHOOSING MATERIALS

A pergola can be built from treated pine or a hard timber such as oregon. When deciding on a wood, consider cost as well as the aesthetic effect you want to achieve. For this pergola we wanted a massive effect and used heavier timbers than would normally be necessary.

In choosing a roofing material, first assess how much shade you need. A pergola on the north or west side of the house may require full protection from the sun, while one on the south may be better open to the weather. You may also choose to use a material that will shelter you from summer rain. Remember, however, not to use a material that will cut down the light or ventilation reaching indoors. See page 20 for a selection of popular roofing materials.

ATTACHING POSTS

If you are adding the pergola to an existing timber deck, locate the posts directly above those that support the deck. Use posts that are about 100 mm longer than the plan calls for, then trim their tops. Secure the new posts with angle brackets or post supports, as shown in diagram 1, top right.

Posts should not rest on a concrete patio that has no footings underneath as the concrete could crack. If building a new patio, pour a concrete footing along with the patio and embed a post support or

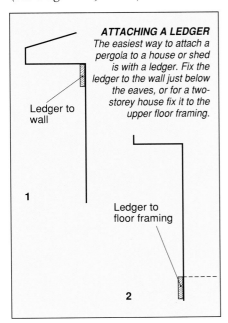

ATTACHING A LEDGER
The easiest way to attach a pergola to a house or shed is with a ledger. Fix the ledger to the wall just below the eaves, or for a two-storey house fix it to the upper floor framing.

Ledger to wall

Ledger to floor framing

1

2

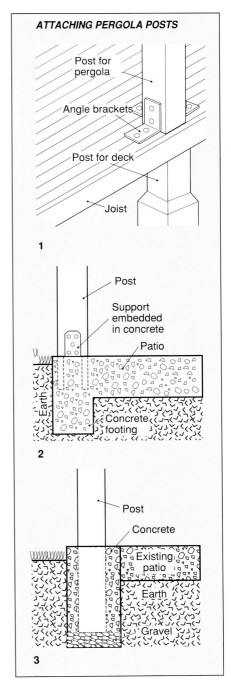

ATTACHING PERGOLA POSTS

Post for pergola

Angle brackets

Post for deck

Joist

1

Post

Support embedded in concrete

Patio

Earth

Concrete footing

2

Post

Concrete

Existing patio

Earth

Gravel

3

ERECTING THE PERGOLA

The basis for most pergolas is the 100 x 100 mm post set firmly into the ground (see page 17). Place the posts so that they do not obstruct access to doorways or block an attractive outlook.

In order to achieve a massive effect for our pergola, we constructed beams by sandwiching a strip of plywood between two 300 x 50 mm timbers to create a member the same size as the 100 x 100 mm post. First nail the plywood to one 300 x 50 mm timber and then nail the beam together from both sides. The plywood is not structurally necessary and can be omitted if you do not require the beam to be precisely flush with the post edges. For a lighter pergola (and one that is cheaper), you can use a single 150 x 50 mm timber for the beam. For the rafters, use 150 x 50 mm. Battens can be 50 x 50 mm or 38 x 38 mm.

As well as timber you will need cement and post supports, and fixings to secure the beam and rafters—either post caps or nail plates (whichever you find most comfortable to work with), and pergola angles. The battens are attached with galvanised nails.

1 Determine post placement. Erect posts (100 x 100 mm) and, if needed, ledger. Transfer a level line from the ledger to the posts or from post to post. Mark cut lines, allowing for rafter and beam thickness.

3 Nail a metal post cap to the top of each post. Or you can bolt the beams to the sides of the posts, or secure with galvanised steel nail plates to both sides of the beams and posts.

4 Construct the beams as is described above or use a 150 x 50 mm timber for a less massive effect. For design interest we shaped the ends of the beam and rafters with a jigsaw.

5 Set the beam into the post caps or fix it to the posts. Use a level to check that it is horizontal, if necessary. Check for square, too. Then drive nails through caps or nail plates into the beam.

7 Attach pergola anchors to the beam and the ledger, if any. For 150 x 50 mm timbers, space the angles 400–600 mm apart, depending on the weight of roofing materials and the water load it must bear.

8 Cut rafters to length and shape their ends with a jigsaw, if desired. Install the rafters level or, to slope them away from the house, measure and cut notches at each end of the rafters, as shown above.

9 Nail through pergola angles into the rafters. Pergola angles will be structurally adequate if you are using rigid roofing material. If not, brace between rafters with short lengths of 150 x 50 mm.

2 Cut the posts to the proper height. Make two passes with a circular saw and remove waste. Don't use a chain saw: standing on a ladder, you won't have enough leverage to operate it safely.

6 Post caps alone won't handle the stress of post and beam connections. Cut diagonal 75 x 25 mm braces and nail them to one or, for stronger support, both sides of the post and beam.

10 Cut 50 x 50 mm battens to length and nail them to the rafters at 100 mm centres, using one as a spacer between battens. For some other roofing possibilities see page 20.

ANATOMY OF A PERGOLA

An attached pergola has a solid ledger (at least 150 x 50 mm) attached to the house and a beam (joist or header) on the other side. The beam rests on posts (usually 100 x 100 mm). Fastened to the ledger and resting on the beams are rafters. Diagonal braces can be used to strengthen the post and beam connection. Shade battens are nailed to the rafters.

A freestanding pergola has posts both sides and two beams, instead of a beam and ledger.

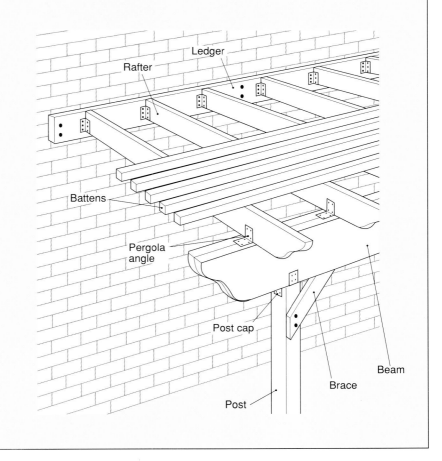

LADDER SAFETY

Getting up on a ladder is potentially dangerous. When using a step ladder, make sure you stand it on a surface that is level and firm and spread the legs widely.

With an extension ladder, the correct slope should be one in four. This means that the feet of the ladder should be placed outside the line of the gutter post, or (if it is leaning against a building) a distance equal to one quarter of the height between the ground and the gutter. Also the top of the ladder should extend at least 1 m above the top of the wall or support and the top half of the ladder should not be extended more than three-quarters of its length.

Again, make sure the extension ladder stands on a firm surface. With both ladders, get someone to hold them while you ascend and descend. Wear shoes with soles that grip (such as sandshoes) and, if you are climbing onto a roof, wait until it is dry before you get up on it.

T-POST PORCH SHADE

This porch is free-standing, although you will need to stabilise it against the wall of your house. Its structural simplicity, stylish appearance and partial shading make it an elegant addition to any house. The alternating long and short battens give an unusual fringed effect to the structure and allow greater interplay of light and shadow. A more regular effect could be achieved by using battens of one length, if that would suit the style of your house. Or you could achieve a more formal look by shaping the ends of the beams and rafters. We used oregon for the superstructure with sawn oregon for the posts.

The height and span of the porch will be determined by your entranceway: if the span is more than 4 m you will need to use heavier timbers than we specify in our materials list. In this porch the T-structure beam is 1800 mm long and stabilised to the fascia board at the eaves. The posts are located no more than half this distance (i.e. 900 mm) out from the fascia board.
1 Dig footing holes and pour two concrete footings (300 x 300 x 300 mm), inserting post supports in each to hold the 100 mm square posts. Check that the supports are in line.

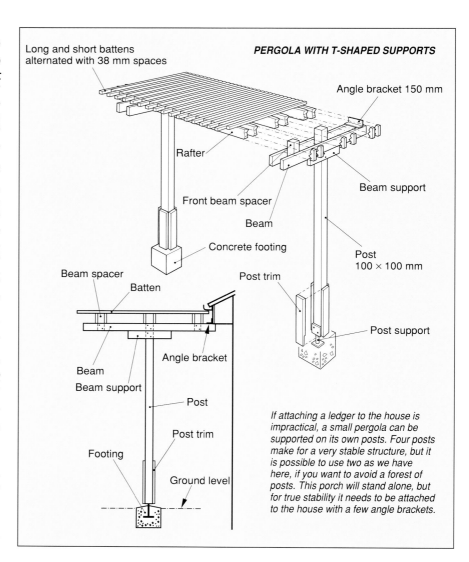

PERGOLA WITH T-SHAPED SUPPORTS

Long and short battens alternated with 38 mm spaces

Angle bracket 150 mm

Rafter

Front beam spacer

Beam support

Beam

Concrete footing

Post 100 × 100 mm

Beam spacer

Batten

Post trim

Beam

Angle bracket

Post support

Beam support

Post

Post trim

Footing

Ground level

If attaching a ledger to the house is impractical, a small pergola can be supported on its own posts. Four posts make for a very stable structure, but it is possible to use two as we have here, if you want to avoid a forest of posts. This porch will stand alone, but for true stability it needs to be attached to the house with a few angle brackets.

Allow the footings to cure for at least one week.
2 Bolt each pair of beams to the posts 150 mm down from the top, using two 200 x 10 mm bolts at each junction. Nail 250 x 100 x 50 mm blocks (beam spacers) between the pairs of beam timbers 200 mm in from each end, flush at the bottom and rising 150 mm above the upper surface. Nail each pair of 600 mm long beam supports to the posts beneath the beams, using 60 mm galvanised nails.
3 Stand the two post structures in their supports and drill and bolt them in place.
4 Use angle brackets to fix one end of each beam to the fascia board and roof frame of the house.

Pergolas make ideal porch covers. This unusual shade has alternating long and short battens for decorative effect.

5 Nail a 150 x 38 mm rafter to either side of the top of the posts, as well as to each side of the spacer blocks protruding between the beams. Nail three rafter spacers, evenly placed along the span, between each of the pairs of rafters.

6 Use 50 mm nails to fix the battens across the top of the rafters, with 38mm spaces between each one. Alternate the long battens with the short ones.

7 To conceal the post supports, chisel out the bottom of the post trims so that they will fit over the metal, and use 100 mm nails to fix the trims to each face of the lower posts. Paint the structure with clear or solid timber preservative.

MATERIALS LIST

Component	Material	Length/size (mm)	Quantity
Post	100 x 100	2700	2
Beam	100 x 38	1800	4
Beam spacer	100 x 50	250	4
Beam supports	100 x 38	600	4
Post trim	100 x 50	600	8
Rafters	150 x 38	3600	6
Rafter spacers	100 x 50	150	9
Battens (long)	38 x 38	1800	24
Battens (short)	38 x 38	1650	24

Other: Two 150 mm angle brackets; two galvanised post supports; four 200 x 10 mm cuphead bolts; packets of 100 mm, 60 mm and 50 mm galvanised bullet-head nails

CREATING A WALKWAY

Interest can be added to a long pathway by building a pergola over it. The longer the structure, the more impact it will have, adding variety to the garden by providing a shadow pattern and a base for climbing plants. Or it can be covered to provide protection from wind or rain.

Use the basic pergola construction described on pages 12–13, adapting it to suit the shape and style of walkway you want. Be sure to make it high enough that drooping vines and climbing plants will not hit the walker, and wide enough for two people to pass comfortably (about 2 m is a good width). If you want to connect rafters and beams with housed joints, see the instructions for the shadehouse on pages 18–19.

Bush logs make an unusual and very effective walkway. Set the posts at least 200 mm into the ground and 3 m apart. Make the walkway 2 m wide and drill and bolt the top rafters in place at 600 mm intervals. Saw 500 mm lengths of logs to 45 degrees and skew nail them in place either side of the top posts so that they form braces.

Bush logs have been used to construct this rustic-effect walkway. They would look well in any informal setting.

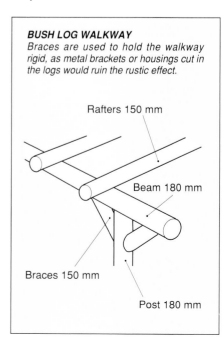

BUSH LOG WALKWAY
Braces are used to hold the walkway rigid, as metal brackets or housings cut in the logs would ruin the rustic effect.

Rafters 150 mm

Beam 180 mm

Braces 150 mm

Post 180 mm

PERGOLA POSTS

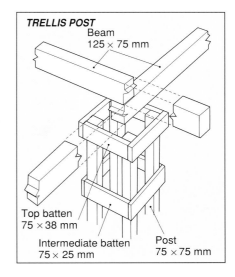

TRELLIS POST
Beam
125 × 75 mm
Top batten
75 × 38 mm
Intermediate batten
75 × 25 mm
Post
75 × 75 mm

Octagonal 'columns' give a more formal look to this pergola.

Most pergolas have plain, unadorned posts that suit the relaxed garden atmosphere, but there are many ways to dress them up. If you want a more formal setting, choose columns to reflect that, or you can be innovative and make your pergola posts a design feature in themselves.

If you want 'columns' rather than mere posts, make them from three 150 x 50 mm timbers. Cut down the length of two timbers, removing

50 mm from each of the outer corners. Fix the cut timbers to either side of the uncut one to form an octagonal column. For an extra flourish, shape the ends of the beams with a jigsaw.

Pergola posts can become structures in themselves. Construct a post with four timber verticals (75 x 75 mm) joined by horizontal battens (75 x 38 mm ones at top and bottom with 75 x 25 mm ones in between) at approximately 500 mm centres to form trellis-like posts that can also serve as supports for a variety of climbing plants.

Right: Trellis-like posts bring the garden right into your pergola.

OCTAGONAL 'COLUMN'
150 × 50 mm

Beam
150 × 38 mm

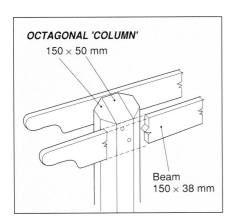

FIXING POSTS AT GROUND LEVEL

There are three main methods of fixing posts.

1 Dig the post hole and place a foundation of gravel or brick rubble in the bottom to provide drainage. Insert the post and add wet or dry concrete mix or tamped earth around it.

2 Provide a concrete base with a pipe partly embedded in the concrete. Drill a hole in the bottom of the post so that it will fit over the pipe. Place damp-course material between the timber and the concrete, or seal the concrete with bitumen paint.

3 Provide a concrete base and embed a post support in it. Fix

the post to the support. In areas where termites are active, this is the preferred post-fixing method.

The size of the footing required will depend on your local conditions (for instance, whether you are building on clay, rock or sand), the post size and type of timber and the roof structure. Check with your local council.

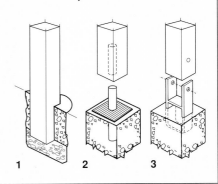

1   2   3

MAKING A SHADEHOUSE

This simple shadehouse has been made by building a narrow pergola along one side of the house and using shadecloth to cover it. Cover as much or as little of the pergola as you need to provide a suitable environment for your shade-loving plants. Our structure is 5 m long, 1.8 m wide and 2.7 m high. Wide rails between the posts serve as shelves for narrow containers.

Our structure is built from oregon and covered with Weathashade Plus shadecloth. Choose a shadecloth to suit your needs (50 or 70 per cent are the densities used by most home owners) in a width that will be most useful. As our pergola is 1800 mm wide we used the 1830 mm width.

1 Follow the directions given in 'Building a pergola' on pages 12–13 to erect the ledger, posts and beam, but before lifting the ledger and beam into position, mark and cut the housings and halving joints for the rafters. In the ledger, mark a 50 mm wide housing at one end and then mark 50 mm housings at 600 mm centres. Cut and chisel out the housings. Measure 450 mm from one end of the beam and then another 50 mm. This marks the first halving joint. Then proceed along the beam, marking 50 mm joints at 600 mm centres. Cut out the joints to a depth of 50 mm. If desired, you can slope the rafters away from the house slightly.

2 Sit the rafters in position and number each one and the corresponding joint. On each one, mark the position of the halving joint, take the rafters down and cut out the joint to a depth of 50 mm. If desired, cut a bevel or use a jigsaw to shape the exposed ends of the rafters. Put the rafters back in place (match the numbers) and nail down.

3 We inserted two rails between the posts; you can determine where you want yours but they should not be more than 1 m apart. Find the centre of one post, mark it and then place another mark 50 mm below it (this gives the housing width for the centre rail). Then measure down another 1 m for the top of the bottom rail and 50 mm for its housing width. Use a level and the rail timber to determine the positions of the housing on the opposite post (the rails/shelves must be level) and mark them. Cut out the housings to a depth of 6 mm.

4 Square one end of each rail, insert it a little way into its housing and then mark its required length at the next post. Square off that end, insert the rail into the housings and nail into position.

Any pergola can be converted to a shadehouse by adding some shadecloth. Here clever use has been made of a long narrow porch.

5 Rails that are to serve as shelves for plants will need a support in the centre (or if your pergola posts are 2400 mm or more apart, you will need to use two supports, evenly spaced). The bottom rail will also need a post support if it is to bear plants. Each support should be 1000 mm long. Nail it through the top rail and skew nail to the bottom.

6 To fix the shadecloth to the roof, first lay a couple of battens across the rafters to help support the shadecloth while you roll it out. If you are using knitted shadecloth, the ends can be fixed directly to the timbers; but if you have chosen a woven fabric, allow enough over-hang all around so that you can double the edges under before fix-ing them. Place one end of the shadecloth roll on one end rafter and fix it to the rafter with the spe-cial fasteners. Then roll the shade-cloth along the loose battens to the other end of the pergola and fix it to the end rafter. Cut off the cloth and remove the loose battens.

7 Smooth the shadecloth over the top of the ledger and either fix it directly to the ledger with special fasteners, or place a batten on the cloth and nail it through to the ledger. Stretch the fabric out to the beam and fix it to the top of the beam in the same way. Use shade-cloth fasteners to fix the cloth to the rafters so that it is secure.

8 Measure the height of the pergola from the base of the rafters where they rest on the beam, to the ground. Cut the shadecloth to slightly over length. Fix one end of the cloth to the beam with fasteners or batten. Stretch the cloth down to the bottom rail and fix it in place. Use shadecloth fasteners to fix the sides of the cloth to the posts. If the cloth is not wide enough to stretch from post to post, you will need to join two lengths by closely sewing them together with a heavy waxed thread, or you may be able to fix the cloth lengthwise.

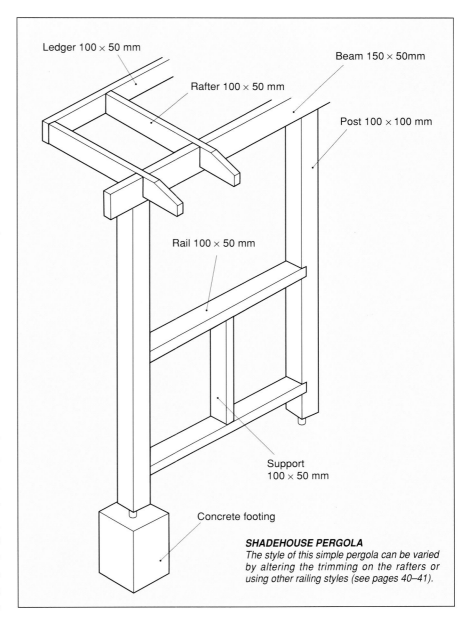

Ledger 100 × 50 mm

Beam 150 × 50mm

Rafter 100 × 50 mm

Post 100 × 100 mm

Rail 100 × 50 mm

Support 100 × 50 mm

Concrete footing

SHADEHOUSE PERGOLA
The style of this simple pergola can be varied by altering the trimming on the rafters or using other railing styles (see pages 40–41).

MATERIALS LIST

Component	Dimensions (mm)	Length (mm)	Quantity
Post	100 x 100	2700	4
Beam	150 x 50	6000	1
Ledger	100 x 50	5000	1
Rafter	100 x 50	1800	9
Rail	100 x 50	2200	2
Support	100 x 50	1000	1

Other: 13.5 m shadecloth, shadecloth fasteners, battens (if desired), two bags ready-mixed concrete, four post supports or brackets, six masonry bolts or coach bolts (to fix ledger to wall), sixteen bolts or framing anchors to fix beam to posts, 75 x 50 mm nails to fix rafters

Photographs and information from Gale Australia Pty Ltd.

ROOFING METHODS

Shade battens: Nail battens (usually 38 x 38 mm) to the rafters, using one batten as a spacer. Use wider or narrower ones and space them according to the amount of shade required or for a decorative effect. Or you can use long and short ones to create a fringed look.

Lattice: Criss-crossed slats of lath offer a lacy effect. The strips can be left to weather, they can be painted, or you can use inexpensive grape-stake lattice, which has a rough, furry texture.

Reed or bamboo: These inexpensive and perishable materials have a limited life span. Prolong their use by rolling them up and storing them inside during winter.

Shadecloth: Meshed fabric coverings provide filtered shade from sunlight, but let air and moisture through. Shadecloth is a maintenance-free alternative to the traditional canvas.

Canvas: Heavy cotton duck provides some protection against rain, but it must be stretched taut so that water won't collect on it.

Fibreglass: Corrugated plastic panels are easy to cut and fix with screws. Slope the canopy so that water will run off.

Vines: Grape vines are the traditional Mediterranean (and Australian!) covering for pergolas, and deciduous creepers continue to be a popular choice. They give shelter from the sun in summer and yet allow the winter sunlight to penetrate.

Strips of canvas are draped over battens placed at 300 mm centres to provide a stylish and unusual covering for this pergola. Fix the canvas to each batten or it will act like a sail in a strong wind!

Shadecloth is an ideal covering for a pergola. It is light, and comes in a range of densities from light shade to extra heavy and in a wide range of colours. Knitted or woven varieties are available.

Plant a grape vine to cover your pergola and you create the perfect atmosphere for outdoor meals and entertaining. Choose wisely and you will also have your own grape supply to eat or use for wine.

GARDEN SHED WITH STYLE

All too often the garden shed is an inelegant structure hidden away at the end of the garden. But build our shed and you'll want it to be where everyone can see it! It will add style to any garden, and it fits well even in a small courtyard.

Our shed measures 4 x 3 m and is 3 m high. It stands on a solid concrete base and has a wooden frame covered with fibro sheeting and a simple corrugated iron roof. The double doors allow easy access and exits for large items such as benches and plenty of light whenever you are working. Although our shed does not have a window, we have provided instructions if you want to include one in your shed. We used some old french doors and lattice panels to achieve a stylish shed without a lot of expense. You can choose to vary the basic structure to suit your taste and budget: Western red cedar cladding and a solid wooden door would give a more rustic look if you have a large country or suburban garden.

A garden shed need not be an ugly addition to the garden. Old patio doors and some lattice make this one both individual and stylish.

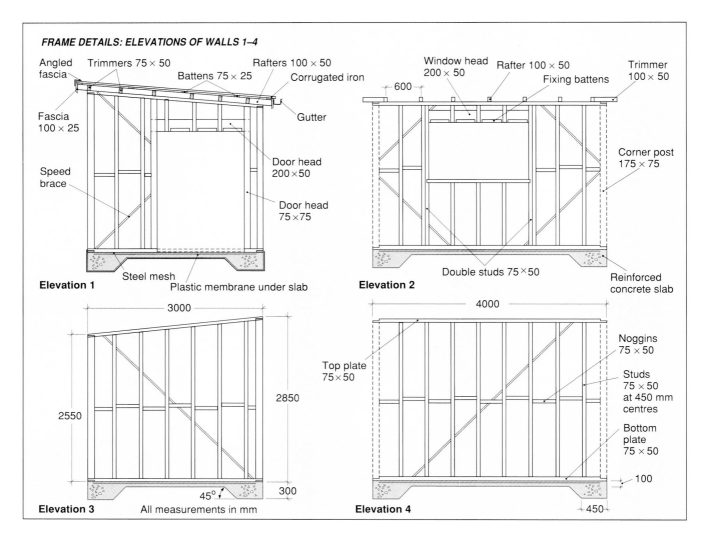

FRAME DETAILS: ELEVATIONS OF WALLS 1–4

Angled fascia
Trimmers 75 × 50
Rafters 100 × 50
Battens 75 × 25
Corrugated iron
Fascia 100 × 25
Gutter
Speed brace
Door head 200 × 50
Door head 75 × 75
Steel mesh
Plastic membrane under slab
Elevation 1

Window head 200 × 50
Rafter 100 × 50
Fixing battens
Trimmer 100 × 50
600
Corner post 175 × 75
Double studs 75 × 50
Reinforced concrete slab
Elevation 2

3000
2850
2550
300
45°
Elevation 3
All measurements in mm

4000
Top plate 75 × 50
Noggins 75 × 50
Studs 75 × 50 at 450 mm centres
Bottom plate 75 × 50
100
450
Elevation 4

BUILDING THE SHED

If possible, select a site for your shed that is already roughly level, or you will need to do a lot of digging to prepare it, and if the site is sloping remember to ensure the door does not face an upward slope or it will be flooded whenever it rains. If you are not an experienced builder, you can choose to subcontract the concrete work and even have the frame ready cut, assembled and delivered directly to your site by a local framemaker.

You will almost certainly need building permission from your local council to erect your shed, and you may need a builder's licence or owner builder's licence, too. If you connect electricity or plumbing to the shed, you will need to call in licensed contractors. Check with your local council before you begin work.

LAYING THE SLAB

1 Measure out the 3 x 4 m slab area on the ground, placing marker pegs at each corner and string lines between them. Use triangulation (see box on page 35) to ensure the lines are square (a good check is to make sure the diagonals are the same length).

2 Dig out the slab area to a depth of 100 mm and ensure that it is level. If the site is sloping, the area should be cut 100 mm into the highest part and you will need to backfill the lower parts of the area to make it level. Then dig out 450 mm wide trenches around the edges of the slab area, to a depth of 300 mm (see elevations). These will hold the concrete footings. Use a level to check the depths of the trenches.

3 Erect formwork for the footings, using boards that are cut to length and close to 300 mm wide. Place them on edge around the edges of the slab area and nail them to the corner stakes. Wherever the boards are not fully supported by the sides of the trenches, hammer in extra stakes along the length of the boards so that they do not bow out when the concrete is poured. Ensure that the corners are very well supported. Make sure there are no gaps at the bottom of the boards where concrete may leak out. Use a level to check that the tops of the boards are level, and use a tape to check that the formwork is square (do this by checking that the parallel sides are the same length and also that the diagonals are the same).

4 Coat the inside faces of the formwork with clean motor oil. This will make it easier later to strip the formwork off.

5 Lay plastic sheeting over the area of the slab and up the inside of the formwork to form a moisture barrier (see elevations). Make sure any joins overlap at least 150 mm.

6 Place the F72 welded steel mesh in position, supported on 50 mm chairs so that it will be in the centre of the concrete slab. The mesh should end 50 mm from the edges of the proposed slab. Be sure there is no rust on the mesh as it could cause concrete cancer.

7 Have the footings inspected by the local council and arrange to have 2.5 m³ of concrete delivered. Ensure you have access for the concrete truck or enough strong wheelbarrows available to transport the concrete. If you are using wheelbarrows, you may need to build a ramp to get them over the formwork—be sure it is strong enough to support the full load without damaging the formwork.

8 Place the concrete in position and push it around with a shovel to ensure that no air is trapped inside the mix. Tamp it in with a 100 x 50 mm timber. Using a straight length of timber long enough to go from one side to the other, begin levelling the concrete by dragging the timber with a sliding action across the slab, filling any low spots as you go and removing any excess from in front of the screed. Always pull towards yourself. Check that the mesh has stayed in position and pull it up if it has been pushed down.

9 To level any imperfections left in the surface and allow excess moisture to rise to the surface and evaporate, use a wooden float, swinging it in wide arcs across the surface, each stroke overlapping with the last. Remove any pieces of aggregate, or push them down into the mix. To reach the centre of the slab you may need to kneel on a large plank placed across the surface: be very careful.

10 Allow the concrete to 'go off', that is, dry sufficiently for the surface water to evaporate and the concrete to harden sufficiently to bear a little weight. (How long it takes depends on the weather.) Then, repeat the floating process with the timber float.

11 If you require a very smooth finish, once the concrete has dried enough that only a very slight mark is made when you push your finger into the slab, give the slab a final float with a steel trowel. When using a steel trowel, pass it over the surface with semi-circular motions, each stroke overlapping the last. The first pass should be made with the trowel flat on the concrete, the second and third with the leading edge of the trowel raised slightly. Finally, run the edge of your trowel around between the formwork and concrete to make it easier to remove the formwork without breaking away the edges of the concrete.

12 Allow the slab to cure for five to seven days. Then remove the pegs (you may need to use a pinch bar). Tap the form boards to release them from the concrete and strip them away.

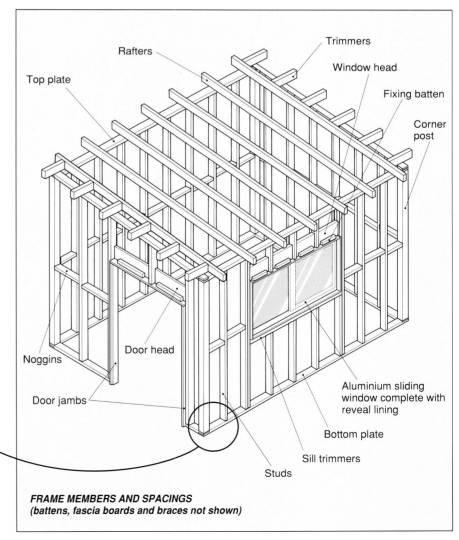

FRAME MEMBERS AND SPACINGS
(battens, fascia boards and braces not shown)

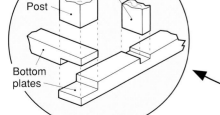

Detail of corner construction

ERECTING THE FRAMEWORK

1 Take two 4.2 m lengths of 75 x 50 mm timber for the top and bottom plates of one long side. Place them side by side (tack them together to keep them aligned) and square them off at one end. Mark the inside face of each (these faces will face each other when erected). Cut them to size so that they are the exact same length as the slab (they may overhang up to 10 mm but no more than that).

2 Working from one end, place a mark at 425 mm, the position of the first stud. Then continue along the length marking at 450 mm intervals (see elevation 4). Place an offcut of the plate material against each mark to mark the other side of each housing (studs will be at 450 mm centres). Cut out each of the housings to a depth of 6 mm. On the top face at each end of both top and bottom plates, prepare lap joints for joining the frame. The cuts are the full width of the plate, 75 mm long and 25 mm deep.

3 Repeat steps 1 and 2 for the other long wall, but provide for double studs on each side of the window (add them on the outer sides of the existing stud marks; see elevation 2). Allow 5 mm space between the double studs and window frame.

Wall 2, showing guttering and down-pipe attached to stormwater drain.

Corner between walls 1 and 2, showing wall 1 fascia board extending beyond the guttering attached to wall 2.

4 Select eight straight pieces of 75 x 50 mm timber for the wall studs of wall 4 and tack them together. Cut them to 2762 mm long. Use 100 mm nails to nail the studs to the top and bottom plates. Cut noggins from 75 x 50 mm timber to fit the stud spacings and nail them into place. It is easier if they are staggered. Square the frame and cut and nail in the diagonal speed brace, as shown on the elevation. If you intend to line your shed, chisel out the studs slightly so that the brace will be flush with them.

5 Select ten studs for wall 2 and cut them to 2462 mm long. Tack them (but do not nail them yet) to the top and bottom plates. Measure up 1 m from the bottom of the frame and draw a line across the double studs and the three studs between them for the sill trimmer. Measure up 1 m from the line and mark another line across the same studs for the bottom of the window head. Cut the three intermediate studs across at the two lines. Cut the sill trimmer 1762 mm long from 75 x 50 mm timber and the head 1950 mm long from 200 x 50 mm. Cut 6 mm deep housings in the double studs for the sill trimmer, and cut housings that go through the full thickness of the studs for the head.

6 Insert sill trimmer and head and nail frame together with 100 mm nails. Insert and nail noggins between the outer studs and cut in two diagonal speed braces, as shown in elevation 2.

7 Stand frames in position and brace them across the top and at each end. Ensure the frames are plumb and parallel and fix them to the slab, using four 100 mm masonry bolts per frame.

8 The end frames can now be made to fit the front and back frames. Set out the bottom plates for walls 1 and 3 together and cut them to length. Mark and cut the lap joints on the ends so that they join with the bottom plates of the long sides. Mark the positions of the stud housings as for the sides. For wall 1 use 75 x 75 mm door studs (or double studs as for the window) 1500 mm apart, on either side of the door (leave the small studs above the door to be inserted later). Cut out the housings. Select stud timbers (each at least 2762 mm long) and nail them in position. Cut and nail in staggered noggins.

9 Place the top plate of wall 3 across the top of the frames for walls 2 and 4, in its final position. Mark and cut out the lap joints. Stand the bottom plate and attached studs in position. Plumb up the frame and use a temporary brace to fix it in position. Mark the required heights and the angles of the cuts needed on the studs and the positions of the housings on the top plate. Lay the frame down and cut the studs and housings. Nail the frame together and add the speed brace. Stand frame back in position and fix it to the slab using 100 mm masonry bolts. Repeat for wall 1.

10 Cut four corner posts to fit between top and bottom plates (the post ends are cut square) and nail them into position.

11 Measure up 2100 mm on each of the door posts. This will be the bottom of the door head. Cut the door head, 1800 mm long, from 200 x 50 mm timber. Cut housings through the thicknesses of the posts for the head and nail it into position. Cut and house small studs for above the door (keeping to maximum 450 mm centres) and nail them in position. Cut 300 x 75 x 25 mm fixing battens to go above the door and window and nail them in place on the heads. (Cladding will be nailed to them.)

ADDING THE ROOF

1 Cut seven 3.6 m long rafters from 100 x 50 mm timber. Find the centre of the top plates of walls 2 and 4 to act as centre for the central rafter. Work out from the central rafter, marking positions of other rafters at 600 mm centres. Place the rafters in position with equal overhang at each end. Mark the positions of bird's mouth cuts where the rafters sit on the top plates. Take the rafters down and cut out the birds' mouths. Replace the rafters and skew nail them to the top plates, using two 75 mm nails on each side of each rafter.

2 Cut twelve trimmers from 100 x 50 mm timber so that each trimmer overhangs the end of the shed by 180 mm. Mark the positions of the trimmers on the top plates of walls 1 and 3 at 600 mm centres, beginning at the wall 4 end. The skew nail the trimmers to the top plates of walls 1 and 3 and nail them firmly to the end rafters.

3 On the end rafters measure out 180 mm from the frame, and then use a string or chalk line to mark the rest of the rafters. Cut the ends plumb (use a sliding bevel). It is important that these cuts be plumb and in line as the fascia boards will be fixed to them.

4 Using 75 mm nails fix 75 x 25 mm battens at right angles to the rafters. The battens should be fixed at 900 mm centres and extend the full length of the roof, from the end of one trimmer to the end of the other. Fix the first batten flush with the top edges of the rafters and finish flush with the bottom edges.

5 Cut two 150 x 25 mm fascia boards to lengths of 3750 mm. Fix the fascia boards to walls 1 and 3. The top of the boards should be flush or slightly under the top of the roof batten and the groove (for the eave lining to fit in) should be level with the bottom of the trimmer. The fascia boards should extend

from the end of the rafters on wall 4 (the high end) to 150 mm beyond the rafter at the wall 2 (lower) end, to accommodate the guttering. Nail them in place using 75 mm nails. Cut two fascia boards to fit between the end fascias and nail them in place. Check that the fascia boards are all parallel and that the corners are square.

6 To fix guttering along wall 2, use 25 mm clouts to nail a gutter bracket through the fascia into a rafter at one end. Then nail a second bracket at the other end (where the drainpipe will be), but ensure it is 12–16 mm lower than the first one. Run a string line between the two brackets and use it as a guide to ensure a regular slope when nailing brackets to each rafter.

7 Use a hacksaw to cut the PVC guttering to length and fix it to the brackets. Using adhesive (see the guttering manufacturer's instructions), fix a drainpipe to the guttering. Be sure the drainpipe connects to a stormwater drain, not to the sewer.

8 Add the corrugated iron roofing sheets, beginning above wall 1 or 3. Place the first sheet flush with the fascia on wall 4 (the high side) and have it overhang the fascia on wall 2 by 50 mm. Check that it is as close as possible to parallel (no more than 40 mm out at the most) and then use 50 mm galvanised roofing screws to fix it in place, starting at the top in the middle corrugation (always fix on the hills, not in the troughs, to prevent leaks) and then fixing at the lower end. Add the next sheet, overlapping one and a half corrugations, and screw through both sheets. Screw the sheets at every batten.

9 Use a pair of pliers or multigrip to bend up the edges of the troughs of the corrugated iron above wall 4, to prevent water being blown up and into the shed during gales. Fix angled flashing over the edges of the roof sheets and fascia above walls 1, 3 and 4, to weatherproof your roof.

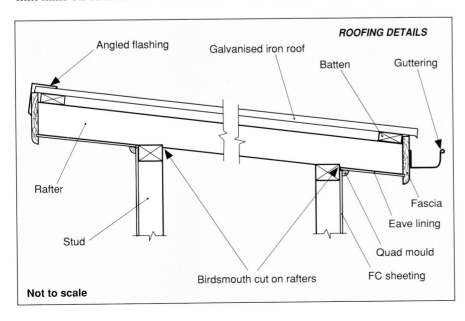

ROOFING DETAILS

Angled flashing

Galvanised iron roof

Batten

Guttering

Rafter

Stud

Fascia

Eave lining

Quad mould

Birdsmouth cut on rafters

FC sheeting

Not to scale

FITTING WINDOW, DOORS AND CLADDING

1 Using flat head clouts, nail a strip of 150 mm flashing (bitumen covered aluminium foil) above the window. This will be bent out to cover the top edge of the window architrave to prevent moisture penetration from above. Place another strip of flashing to form a tray on the sill trimmer for the window to sit in. Sit the window in the opening and bend the flashing up around the bottom and ends of the window on the inside. Adjust the window so that the reveal lining (the outside edge of the window) will finish flush with the cladding, and pack the bottom and sides so that it sits square.

2 Check that the window opens and shuts as it should. Nail through the side reveal linings with four nails each side but don't hammer the nails home in case you need to adjust the positioning later. Be sure the nails have gone through the packing and into the studs to hold the window securely.

3 Attach flashing above the doorway, as for the window.

4 Attach the cladding, beginning with wall 4. Measure the wall height and add 50 mm for the overhang on the concrete slab. Mark and cut the first sheet to length. Line the sheet up with the corner of the wall to be covered, butting it closely to the rafters, and fix it at the top and then down the centre stud. Space the nails about 450 mm apart across the top and 600 mm apart down the centre. Fix the plastic jointing strip down the edge and then nail the edge of the sheet. Prepare and fix the second sheet and so on until the wall is covered.

5 Repeat the operation for the other three walls but do not clad the areas above the window and doors yet.

6 Cut the bottom plate at the door stud junction. Measure your doors. Ours are each 2040 mm high by 720 mm wide and 40 mm thick. Cut the head of the door jamb 1500 mm long to fit the side door jambs. On the lower face of the head jamb, cut a rebate 40 mm wide and 12 mm deep at each end (see detail on figure at left).

7 Cut the side jambs to 2065 mm length, fit them into the side housings on the jamb head and nail the jamb set together. Tack a piece of timber across the side jambs near the bottom (to keep jambs parallel) and tack diagonal braces across the corners to keep the frame square.

8 Place the jamb frame into the door opening, leaving a 5–10 mm gap all around, and use the braces to ensure the frame is flush with the cladding. Pack the sides of the door jambs so that they are straight and plumb and the head is level. Check that the frame is not twisted. Nail the jambs into position (but don't drive the nails home in case you have to adjust them when the doors are fitted) but don't put any nails into the head. Check that the doors will open outwards.

9 Working on both doors at once, mark the position of the hinges. Chisel out the waste and insert the hinges. Hold the door up to the door jamb (use a wedge to raise it to the appropriate height off the ground) and mark the position of the hinges on the jamb. Chisel out the recesses and fix the hinges.

10 Bevel the closing edges of the two doors slightly to prevent them

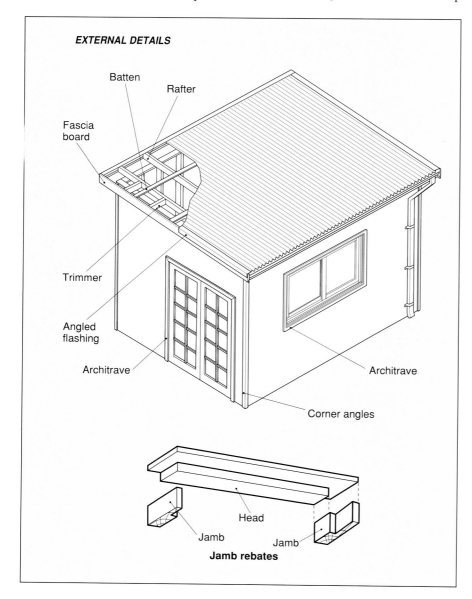

EXTERNAL DETAILS

Batten
Rafter
Fascia board
Trimmer
Angled flashing
Architrave
Architrave
Corner angles

Head
Jamb
Jamb
Jamb rebates

from binding. The door edges should not quite touch on the outside face and should be slightly further apart on the inside. Fix a strip down the outside face of one door to form a closing or weather strip. This will also align the doors when they are closed.

11 Check that the doors open and close easily and adjust the door or jambs as necessary. Complete nailing of the jambs and ensure the nails go right through the packing to keep it in place.

12 Fix a lock to the doors, following the manufacturer's instructions.

13 Fit 75 x 25 mm architraves around the window and doorway, leaving only 5 mm of the door jamb and window reveal linings showing. Keep the bullnose or splay facing the opening. Mitre the corners and fit the vertical architraves first. Pack behind the top pieces to keep them flush with the cladding. At the bottom of the window, the flashing should go in front of the cladding but behind the architrave; at the top of the window and around the door it goes behind the cladding and in front of the architrave.

14 Place the cladding in position above the doors and window. Cut and fit the corner angles at the four corners of the shed.

15 Cut the strips of fibro sheeting to line the eaves. Ensure they are wide enough to fit into the groove on the back of the fascia board. Mark the positions of the rafters on the fascia board and cladding as a guide, and nail the eaves sheets to the rafters. Use plastic joining strips to connect the sheets. Nail lengths of quad moulding in the corner between the eave and the wall.

FINISHING THE SHED

Paint the shed, including door and window frames, in colours to suit your garden. If desired, finish it by fixing battens to the cladding and attaching lattice panels to them. See pages 82–5 for lattice.

MATERIALS LIST

Component	Dimensions (mm)	Length (mm)	Material	Quantity
Frame				
Plates (side walls)	75 x 50	4200	oregon*	4
Bottom plates (end)	75 x 50	3000	oregon	2
Top plates (end)	75 x 50	3300	oregon	2
Studs	75 x 50	2762	oregon	17
Studs	75 x 50	2462	oregon	10
Corner posts	75 x 75	2750		2
Corner posts	75 x 75	2450		2
Door studs	75 x 75	2762		2
Sill trimmer	75 x 50	1762		1
Window head	200 x 50	1950		1
Door head	200 x 50	1800		1
Noggins	75 x 50	425		24
Speed braces		3000		6
Door jamb head	100 x 38	1500	Pacific maple	1
Door jambs	100 x 38	2100	Pacific maple	2
Fixing battens	75 x 25	400		6
Architraves	75 x 25	as req'd	Pacific maple**	
Door closing strip	50 x 25	2100	Pacific maple	1
Roof				
Rafters	100 x 50	3600		7
Trimmers	100 x 50	500		12
Battens	75 x 25	4500		5
Fascia boards	150 x 25	3750		2
Fascia boards	150 x 25	4500		2
Quad moulds	25 x 25	4200		2
	25 x 25	3300		2

*All oregon used is rough sawn. If desired, substitute dimensioned radiata pine instead.
**Bullnosed or splayed

Other:
Slab: 2.5 m³ ready-mixed concrete, two 2950 x 1500 mm F72 welded steel mesh and twelve 50 mm chairs, boards for formwork and sixteen pegs. **Frame:** fourteen 100 mm masonry bolts, six packets 100 mm jolt head nails for framing, two packets 75 mm jolt head nails, one packet 50 mm jolt head nails, 30 mm flat head clouts. **Roof:** five sheets 3600 x 900 mm corrugated iron (Custom Orb or Colour Bond) sheets, one packet 50 x 8 mm galvanised roofing screws, 10.5 m of 150 x 100 mm angled flashing, fifteen sheets of 3000 x 900 x 6 mm FC (fibro) cladding, 36 m plastic joining strips, 12 m of 50 mm plastic corner angle cladding. **Guttering:** 4.5 m of 100 mm PVC guttering, seven gutter brackets, two stop ends, two 45° 100 x 50 mm elbows, 3 m of 100 x 50 mm downpipe, three 100 x 50 astrigals, one 100 x 50 mm rainwater head. **Door:** two french doors (2040 x 720 x 40 mm), two pairs butt hinges (three if the door is heavy), lock. **Window:** aluminium sliding window, 1740 x 990 mm (including reveals), one roll 150 mm Alcor (bitumen covered aluminium foil) flashing, sliding window lock.

DECKS

Every garden needs a level place with a firm floor where you can sit out at any time it isn't raining and have a cup of tea (or something stronger, if you wish). It can be a terrace paved with bricks, stone or whatever, but there are some advantages in building a timber deck. First, a deck is lighter work. You don't have to shift large amounts of earth to get your finished surface level, timber is lighter and easier to handle than paving materials and you don't have to worry about the fall of the ground and drainage. It's a good sort of project to start on if you are not yet confident of your building skills—it's very basic carpentry.

A deck has the added advantage over hard paving that it does not have to be at ground level—you can raise it to just the right height so that you can step straight out of the living room to the garden. If your garden slopes, you can arrange the deck without having to shift earth and build retaining walls—and a multi-level outdoor living room becomes easy.

We haven't made as much use of decks in Australia as the Americans have, partly for fear of termites: but they won't munch on treated pine (use it for the hidden structure) and there are no timbers better for the decking boards, handrails and trim than our own hardwoods. Most decks here are built from hardwoods with sawn or nominal sizes of 75 x 25 mm and 100 x 25 mm. Take a look at pages 35 and 40 for more on selecting timber.

Check with your local council or building authority to make sure the timbers you have selected are suitable and that the spans between bearers and joists are within the recommended range. And remember that any structure higher than fence height requires council permission.

Grass is beautiful but it can be damp underfoot and uncomfortable to sit on. A timber deck will allow you to sit and enjoy the garden without damaging the lawn or getting muddy feet.

GROUND-LEVEL DECKS

Decks need not be large, flat expanses of timber. Here a series of low decks step down a gentle slope, acting both as pathways and as areas for sitting and entertaining. The different shapes add interest to the garden landscape.

A ground-level deck, which stands on its own just a few centimetres above the ground, is considerably easier to build than a raised deck. The simple design of a ground-level deck spares you the intricacies of constructing stairs, railings and structural bracing. And a freestanding, ground-level deck does not need to be securely attached to the structure of the house.

A ground-level deck can be situated just about anywhere: adjacent to the house, or anywhere in the yard where you like to sit. Build one over an existing too-small patio, or stair-step them down a gentle slope. And, like any deck, a ground-level one can be dressed up with railings, benches or a pergola.

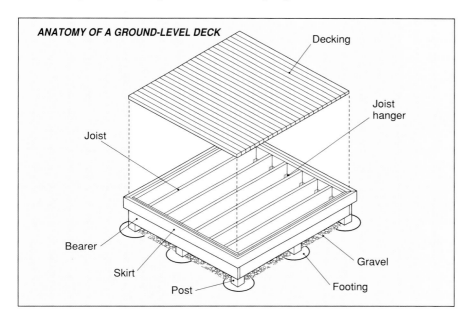

ANATOMY OF A GROUND-LEVEL DECK

Decking

Joist hanger

Joist

Bearer

Skirt

Post

Gravel

Footing

GETTING STARTED

A sturdy deck begins with a sound plan and good quality timber. Sketch out the plan you want and consult your local council or building authority to determine the dimensions of timber you should use, and to ensure you have spaced the bearers and joists properly. Calculate the lengths required, adding 10 per cent for waste. Timbers such as oregon, Western red cedar or treated pine are suitable timbers to use for your deck, and various Australian hardwoods can also be used.

When selecting timber, examine each piece and reject any that are split or badly twisted. Boards with minor warping or cupping, however, will straighten out as they are nailed in place.

A ground-level deck is supported by posts resting on concrete footings (see page 17 for erecting posts) or by wooden piers. Bearers rest on the posts and metal hangers connect joists to the bearers. Decking boards are nailed to the joists. If desired, a board can be added around the edge of the decking to create a neat finish for the deck.

ORDERING TIMBER

You will have much less trouble ordering timber if you are well organised and present the information in a way the timber supplier will recognise. Decide exactly what you need:
- the species, e.g. radiata pine or Pacific maple
- the grade (for load-bearing work such as bearers, joists or beams), e.g. F7
- the condition, e.g. rough sawn or dressed (see box on page 40)
- the section size, e.g. 100 x 50 mm
- the stock length, e.g. 2.7 m
- the number of lengths

You will then be able to prepare an order, such as:

300 x 50 mm rough sawn seasoned oregon F8 grade, 1/4.2 m

250 x 38 mm rough sawn radiata pine unseasoned, 1/2.4 m

Always select the timbers yourself so that you can check for bowing, large knots or splits. This is easier if the timber yard is well organised, with the same species of timber stored together. Always get three quotes as timber prices vary greatly between suppliers.

FASTENERS

Decks seem to eat nails. For every 1 m² of deck, you'll need 125 g of 100 mm nails (for joists) and 250 g of 50 mm bullet-head nails (for decking). Use only galvanised nails; ordinary steel rusts and will stain the timber.

Bolts, nuts, washers and screws also should be galvanised. Bolts should be as long as the total thickness of the materials being joined, plus 20 mm. Screws should be long enough so that two-thirds of their length goes into the member you are fastening to.

1 For a preview of how your deck will look, test-assemble a section. This also gives you a chance to identify your straightest timber. Cut scraps of 10 mm thick timber to serve as spacers between boards.

2 Lay out the site with stakes and string. Here we're marking the location of an intermediate post. Measure diagonals to ensure that corners are square and fix them by erecting batter boards.

3 Excavate so that the deck will sit just above ground level. A marked board indicates the combined height of the deck materials (top), the ground level and height of the posts above the excavated level.

5 Let the concrete cure for a day or two; then mark the tops of posts (use a spirit level and straight edge) on all four faces and cut them off with a circular saw, making them all a level height.

6 Clear the excavated area of vegetation; then, to inhibit vegetation growth, spread polyethylene on the area the deck will cover. Top this with crushed rocks or gravel. Omit the plastic if desired.

7 Construct bearers by nailing two 200 x 50 mm timbers together. Lay the bearers on top of the posts, insert a metal ant cap, and check for level. Attach with galvanised hoop iron (shown) or special brackets.

9 Cut joists to length. Before installing them, sight along each and determine which edge has a bow. Nail joists in place, bowed side up; the weight of the decking will flatten them out.

10 Also nail decking boards to the joists bowed face up. Skew nail at least two nails into each joist, maintaining uniform gaps between boards with spacers. Stagger end-to-end joints.

11 Once all the boards are installed, snap a chalk line along the deck's edge, tack down a timber strip to serve as a guide for the circular saw's table, and cut the boards flush.

4 Dig post holes, pour 50 mm of gravel into the bottom, and set posts in place. Plumb and brace each post and shovel in concrete. Bevel the top of the concrete so that water drains away from the post.

8 Position the joists. Use a scrap of timber to adjust the placement of the joist hangers on the bearers so that the joist tops will fit flush with the bearer tops. Nail the hangers on to the bearers.

12 A board covers the ends of the deck boards and adds a decorative touch. We shaped the top edge of this one with a router, and used a saw to mitre joints at corners and scarfs.

This small deck can be built anywhere in the garden, to take advantage of shade from trees and shrubs or to cover bare or rocky patches.

AN EASY-BUILD DECK

This simple platform will make a favourite spot in your garden extra-special. It will end the annoyance of getting grass stains on clothes or sitting on damp soil. The deck sits on beams that rest on the ground and can be built around a favourite tree, shrub or large, sheltering rock—wherever you like.

1 Select your site carefully to provide impact, shade and shelter.

2 Lay out the timbers so that you can visualise the finished project.

3 Position the 100 x 100 mm bearers (see diagram). If you are building on level ground, only two bearers are needed. Note: Use cedar or treated pine for members touching the ground.

4 Construct the frame of 150 x 50 mm timber as illustrated.

5 Lay decking boards. Fit them closely to the tree trunks but do not attach them to the trees.

6 Stain or apply preservative.

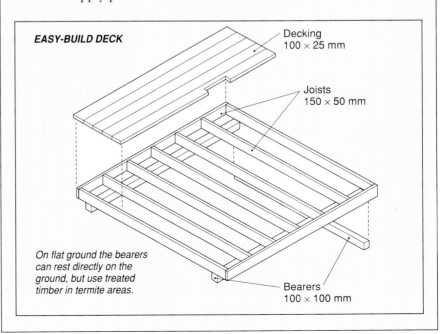

EASY-BUILD DECK

Decking
100 × 25 mm

Joists
150 × 50 mm

On flat ground the bearers can rest directly on the ground, but use treated timber in termite areas.

Bearers
100 × 100 mm

RAISED DECKS

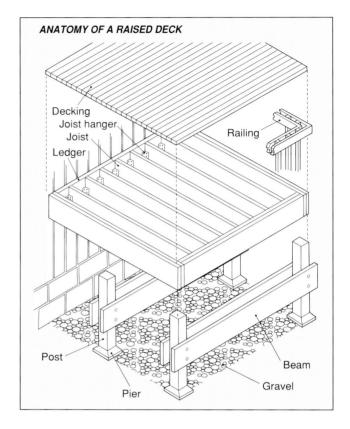

ANATOMY OF A RAISED DECK

Decking
Joist hanger
Joist
Ledger
Railing
Post
Beam
Pier
Gravel

Although more formidable to construct than ground-level decks, raised decks can be built by a do-it-yourselfer equipped with a hammer, circular saw, electric drill and socket wrench set. The wrenches are used for tightening bolts, which will provide more strength than nails and are used at critical points of the structure.

One of these critical points is the ledger that fastens the deck to your house and serves as the deck's starting point. This board must be absolutely level and securely fastened to the floor framing with 150 mm coach screws spaced 600 mm apart. To attach a ledger to a masonry wall, drill holes with a masonry bit and use masonry bolts.

Timber decks with simple vertical railings (see pages 36–7) are the perfect choice for extending the living areas of this house into its bushland setting.

STAIRS AND RAILINGS

Stairs are necessary for any deck more than 200 mm above the ground. If the deck is more than 1 m high, you should also provide a handrail at least 865 mm high, with no more than 200 mm between horizontal rails or vertical balusters. Generally a flight of stairs consists of a number of steps. The vertical height of each step is the 'rise' and the horizontal dimension is the 'going'. To ensure stairs are safe, building codes require that the relationship between rise and going conforms to a formula: 2 rises + 1 going = 585–700 mm. The average rise should be between 150 and 180 mm. (If the risers vary in height more than about 5 mm, people may stumble on them.) Measure the total rise and calculate a suitable rise and

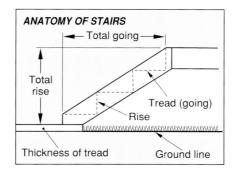

ANATOMY OF STAIRS

going, then determine the total going, remembering there will always be one less going than there are rises. If there are restrictions on space, adjust the rise and going but keep within the formula. If there are more than eighteen steps, you will need a landing.

To attach railings, extend the posts above the decking or bolt verticals to the deck beams (see pages 36–37). See pages 40–1 for more on railings.

TRIANGULATION

When laying out structures, the easiest way to get a right angle is to use triangulation. If you have a triangle with sides in a ratio of 3:4:5, the angle between the 3 and the 4 will always be a right angle. Use a tape and any multiples of 3, 4 and 5 (e.g. 300, 400 and 500 mm, or 600 mm, 800 mm and 1 m) to check for square.

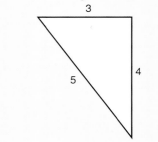

SELECTING TIMBER

Construction timbers are used for most building work. They include the following:

■ oregon, imported from the United States
■ radiata pine, produced in Australia
■ Australian hardwoods, such as blackbutt, turpentine and jarrah

Construction category timbers are graded according to their usual appearance and their structural strength. The best grades for framing timbers are the so-called select merchantable, which has fewer defects such as knots and splits,

and merchantable. Standard building grades are suitable for framing work that will be covered by plasterboard or other wall lining.

For sub-floor framing (bearers and joists) use stress-graded timber. These are graded according to their structural integrity (strength): the higher the grade, the greater the load-bearing capacity. For example, for a non-load bearing floor such as a deck, you should use F5–F8, with F5 being the minimum requirement and F8 the most suitable for the majority of work.

Joinery timbers are used for detailed work such as window and

door frames and other fitments. They include:

■ Western red cedar, imported from the United States
■ Douglas fir (oregon), imported from the United States
■ Tasmanian oak
■ Tasmanian blackwood
■ Pacific maple, imported from Asia and the Pacific region
■ other imported timbers such as teak, walnut and mahogany

Always buy seasoned timber if possible. Otherwise the timbers may split, warp or bow after they have been fixed in place. For more on timber, see 'Timber conditions' on page 40.

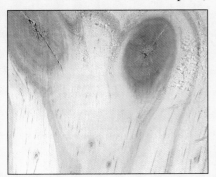

Radiata pine

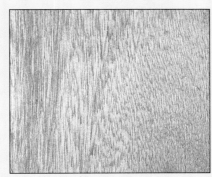

Pacific maple

Western red cedar

1 Test assemble the deck. Then, starting at the house, lay out the site with string, driving stakes where posts will be located. Use a tape measure and the principle of triangulation to ensure the layout is square. It is worth taking extra time now to make sure it is square.

2 Mark the ledger's position by measuring down from the door threshold. Locate the finished deck surface 20–25 mm beneath the sill, so that rain water won't back up into the house. The upper dotted line represents the top of the decking, the lower the top of the ledger.

3 Use a level to make markings because the house or sill may be out of level. Attach the ledger by fastening 100–150 mm coach screws through the cladding into the house floor framing. Fit the coach screws with washers and caulk under them just before tightening.

7 Measure down the posts the height of the joists and mark them to give the position of the top of the bearer. Now use bolts to attach bearers to each side of the posts. We drilled holes and ran the bolts all the way through the post and both bearers. Remember to use washers and check that the bolts are tightly fixed.

8 Space the joist hangers along the ledger and fix them securely to it. Nail the joists in place, fixing them to the ledger and the bearers. We chose to skew nail the joists to the bearer tops, but you can attach the joists with hangers. If you use hangers, the joists will be flush with the bearers and the bearers should be level with the ledger.

9 We used double joists at edges and ends for extra strength, but single ones would be adequate. We notched the posts to carry the outer joists and skew nailed the inner ones between ledger and post and between post and post. As an alternative to notching, extend the bearer beyond the post, rest the joists on it, then nail it to the post.

13 Drill holes, then use bolts to fasten the top stair spacer to the edge joist. You can also attach stairs with metal stairway hangers, or use coach screws to attach the stringers to the ends of joists.

14 Install decking, starting at the house to ensure a snug fit under the sill. Lay decking with the bowed side up. Hold spacers between boards, and then drive two nails into each joist. Trim the ends.

15 We nailed a Western red cedar board around the perimeter joists, bored holes through it and the joists, and then fastened the railing balusters to it with bolts.

4 Dig post holes at stake points, sink and plumb posts, and pour concrete around them. Build a form around the posts to raise the footing; this keeps grass and other vegetation away from the bases of the posts. Bevel the tops of footings to shed water.

5 To determine the correct level of the tops of the posts for cutting, use a straight edge and spirit level, with the straight edge resting on the top of the ledger. Mark the post clearly. Use a combination square to bring the cut-off line around all four faces of each post.

6 Cut the posts to the correct size with a circular or chain saw. If you want the bearers to finish flush with the posts, you will need to set the edge joists into the posts. The face marked here with an X will be notched to catch half of the edge joist (see step 9).

10 Build and install stairs before attaching decking boards. If you are not restricted in the total length (run) of the staircase, measure its height (rise) and multiply by 1 1/3 to determine the run. If your run is restricted, calculate the size of the goings and risers according to the section on stairs and railings given on page 35.

11 Purchase precut stair strings or lay out your own with a square. Cut one string with a circular saw, and then use it as a pattern for laying out the second. Be sure to subtract the thickness of a tread from the bottom riser so that steps will come out equal in height. Uneven risers will cause someone to stumble and may cause accidents.

12 Assemble the staircase by nailing spacer boards at the top and bottom of the strings. Nail treads to all but the top step; wait until you've installed the decking before nailing the final tread. You'll need to pour a concrete footing for the base of the stairway or bolt it to a precast pad so that it doesn't move.

16 To make the rail more comfortable to use, round rail edges with a router or buy routed timber. Drill holes and then drive coach screws through the balusters into the rail.

TOOLS FOR OUTDOOR CARPENTRY
There are few tools required for outdoor carpentry that you won't already have in a basic tool kit. There are, however, a few that will make your work much easier.
- a spirit level about 1 m long for use on large structures
- a large steel square with sides about 600 mm long
- an adjustable bevel, especially for jobs such as sloping the ends of pergola beams or rafters
- a steel tape, which should be   at least 8 m long
- a sturdy wood chisel about 50 mm wide
- a panel saw for cutting structural timbers
- a jigsaw, a power tool for cutting curves and fiddly shapes or bevels
Remember, too, to keep all your cutting tools very sharp.

DECK OUT A STEEP SLOPE

Decks are the ideal solution for those 'wasted' spots in your yard. This cleverly designed deck turns a steep bank into a handsome niche, and at the same time provides a passage from the paved patio to the level below. The distinctive railing is used to unify the deck and the stairway leading to the lower level.

The frame consists of a number of 200 x 50 mm bearers resting on the patio at one end and on two 100 x 100 mm posts at the other end. However, if you are in an area where termites are active, don't rest the bearers directly on the patio: rest them on short posts set in metal post supports

The decking is of 75 x 25 mm Western red cedar, capped with a 50 x 50 mm Western red cedar strip to finish the structure neatly.

Hint
Save effort by buying timber cut to length at the timber yard, but remember to buy longer posts if you are setting them in concrete instead of in post supports.

A combination of deck and stairs is used here to connect two levels of the garden. The whole is unified by the distinctive railing.

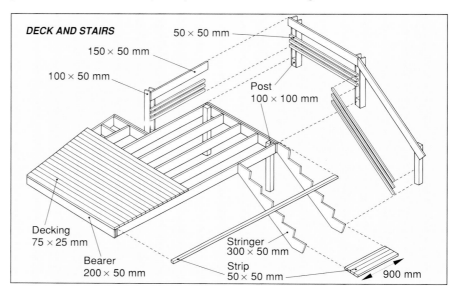

DECK AND STAIRS
- 50 × 50 mm
- 150 × 50 mm
- 100 × 50 mm
- Post 100 × 100 mm
- Decking 75 × 25 mm
- Bearer 200 × 50 mm
- Stringer 300 × 50 mm
- Strip 50 × 50 mm
- 900 mm

SURROUND YOUR POOL

Decking can provide the perfect way to provide easy access to any swimming pool, especially an above-ground pool. This above-ground pool was installed on a steeply sloping site where it would have been difficult and expensive to build an in-ground one. The stepped deck allowed the pool to be integrated into the site and provided several comfortable areas for relaxing and informal entertaining.

A deck is also the perfect place to install a spa, perhaps with inbuilt benches and a screen for privacy. The principles of deck building are always the same.

A deck is the most practical way to surround an above-ground pool.

DECKING STYLES

Decking boards can be laid in a number of different styles. Choose one that suits the shape of your deck and gives it the character you want it to have. But be sure to use a suitable framing pattern to support it.

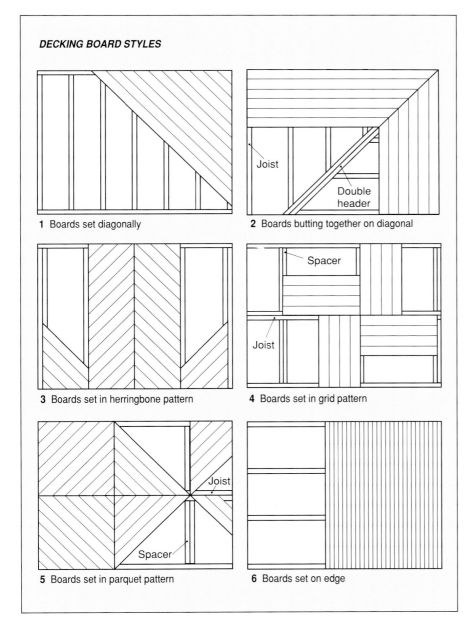

DECKING BOARD STYLES

1 Boards set diagonally

2 Boards butting together on diagonal
- Joist
- Double header

3 Boards set in herringbone pattern

4 Boards set in grid pattern
- Spacer
- Joist

5 Boards set in parquet pattern
- Joist
- Spacer

6 Boards set on edge

1 Trim ends of decking boards at 45 degree angles and install them diagonally to the house instead of parallel. Using a table saw makes the repetitive angle cuts easier and more accurate, or you can make a jig for your portable power saw.

2 Some decking patterns require different framing plans. In this example, butting boards at a diagonal calls for the installation of a double header from corner to corner of the deck.

3 For a herringbone pattern, double the joists and space them 600 mm apart. Cut board ends at 45 degree angles and install them in alternating directions.

4 Grid-pattern decking requires spacers nailed between joists. Additional framing increases the weight—and cost—of a deck, so be sure to plan a substructure that can carry the load.

5 A parquet effect can be created using the same framing plan as for grid-pattern decking.

6 For a superstrong (but expensive!) deck, skew nail 100 x 50 mm boards set on edge. To calculate the number you'll need, take the width of the deck in millimetres and divide by the thickness of one board plus one space.

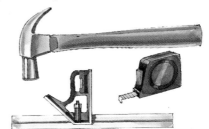

RAILING STYLES

Frame your favourite view in lattice with a combined rail/screen.

Simple vertical slats can be used in a variety of ways within the garden, while allowing you to maintain one overall style.

TIMBER CONDITIONS

Timber in Australia is sold in three basic conditions:

- sawn or rough sawn, which has been brought to a specific (nominal) size by a band saw
- dressed, either dressed-all round (DAR), dressed on two sides (D2S) or double-dressed (DD)
- milled, which is dressed to a specific profile for architraves, window sills, skirting boards and so on

Dressed timber is sold using the same nominal dimensions as sawn timber, for example 100 x 50 mm, but the surfaces have all been machined down to a flat, even width and thickness so that, in fact, the 100 x 50 mm timber will measure 91 x 41 mm. The chart below shows the differences in measurements for seasoned timber; those for some radiata pine timbers will vary, especially timbers larger than 100 x 50 mm.

Milled timbers are also ordered by their nominal sizes. Their finished sizes will generally compare with those given in the chart for dressed timber, but you should check these materials carefully at the timber yard as there will be many variations.

Timber is now sold in stock lengths, which usually begin at 1.8 m and increase by 300 mm increments to 2.1 m, 2.4 m and so on. Short lengths and offcuts are also usually available.

See page 35 for notes on selecting timbers for particular jobs.

Sawn or nominal size (mm)	Finished size after dressing (mm)
10	6
13	9
16	12
19	15
25	19
31	23
38	30
50	41
75	66
100	91
125	115
150	138
175	160
200	185
225	210
250	231
300	281

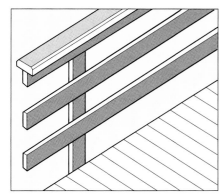

Horizontal railings can be made from three 100 x 50 or 150 x 50 mm boards capped with a 150 x 50 mm handrail. Bolt the verticals and rails together; nail the handrail on after chamfering its edges.

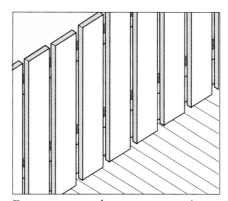

For a screen that ensures privacy but lets in cooling breezes, space 200 x 25 mm timbers 50 mm apart. Nail all boards to one side of the rails, or alternate them on opposite sides for design interest.

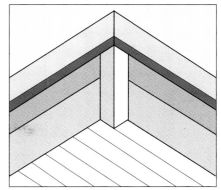

On low decks, build a low, solid railing of horizontal 200 x 50 mm timbers capped with 150 x 50s. Keep the solid railing less than about 600 mm high, or wind will play havoc with it.

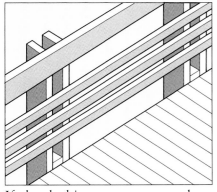

If the decking posts are not long enough to reach railing height, extend them by bolting a 150 x 50 mm board to each side; then nail 50 x 50 and 150 x 50 rail materials to the extensions.

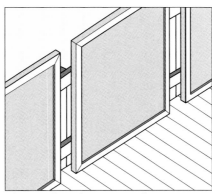

Plywood makes a good contemporary-looking railing. Frame 900 mm square panels with 50 x 25 mm timbers. Space the panels 100 mm apart. Or use laminated glass, lattice or fibre cement sheeting.

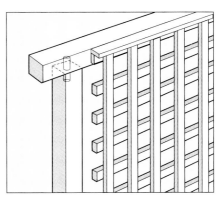

Lattice can be used to provide a decorative screen at the edge of the deck. Fix it to a framework of 100 x 100 mm timbers. Also see pages 82–5 for further instructions on using lattice.

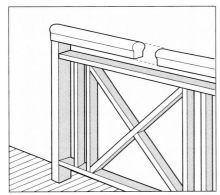

Use cross-braced panels to close the gap between handrail and deck. Make the panels from 100 x 25 mm timbers, the handrail can be made from a 100 x 100 mm timber that is routed to shape.

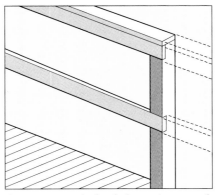

Create a rustic look by using rough sawn timber in a classic post-and-rail style. Notch the post first and then attach the railings with screws. Use 100 x 100 mm posts and 100 x 38 mm railings.

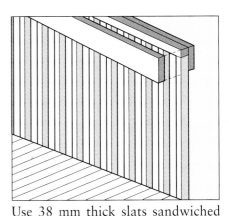

Use 38 mm thick slats sandwiched between more substantial 100 x 38 mm timbers to achieve a railing or screen that provides privacy and shelter from winds. Vary the height to suit your garden.

SMALL PROJECTS

Just as in the house, so in the garden the finishing touches make a great difference. Of course, you'll arrange your plants and flowers with telling effect, but don't overlook the opportunities such details as seating, the letterbox, planters and window boxes can give to add a personal note. None of these projects needs much time to build—you could do just about all of them in a weekend—and none requires more than the most basic skills. Any of the projects would be a good starter before you tackle something more ambitious, and all of them are useful items: we've tested them all and there are no 'why on earth did I make that?' things here.

Most useful of all for some people would be a barbecue, and we have given you two designs to choose from: a simple structure that will nevertheless cook to perfection and one with built-in storage cupboard and worktop. For all their sophisticated design, they aren't at all difficult to build—you should get the hang of laying bricks on a small scale like this in no time, and the grills and hotplates can be bought ready made quite cheaply. Remember to build away from foliage that could catch fire but near your eating area, and take note of prevailing winds—you don't want every barbecue ruined when smoke blows into your house, or into your neighbour's. Sausages, anyone?

A square of simple slatted benches provides a useful focus for outdoor entertaining. Build it with or without the deck and firepit shown here—it will work equally well on grass or paving.

These simple cantilevered seats form a little nook, a perfect spot for conversation or just relaxing alone. They also provide a neat finish to the edge of the deck, dividing it from the open garden beyond.

BUILDING A DECK BENCH

Provide one or more comfortable benches on your deck and see how much more often you use it. Orient benches so that they face an attractive view or face away from one that's not. And choose a style to suit your deck: a backless bench will block less of the view from a ground-level deck, but on a raised deck you can incorporate the back of a bench into the railing. Use the same timbers as for your deck to achieve an integrated project.

BENCH BASICS

Plan the size of your bench carefully, using the dimensions given below in 'Standard bench dimensions'. The height of the back can be adjusted so that it doesn't block a view or to provide privacy or shelter from wind. Open, slatted construction lets air circulate and discourages water from forming pools.

You can secure benches to the same posts that support the deck or fasten uprights to joists. They can also be fixed to the decking. For safety, be sure to use bolts, not nails, at all critical structural points. Benches need not, however, be permanently attached to the deck. Freestanding benches built of the same materials as the deck can be easily moved around to accommodate different functions. Those on high decks should, of course, be butted against a firmly attached railing for safety's sake.

When planning your benches, think about how they could be integrated with other structures. For example, two benches and a table could be built in booth style, or a trellis or pergola could be added above the bench.

STANDARD BENCH DIMENSIONS

A bench seat should be 400–450 mm wide, 400–450 mm from the ground and about 600 mm of length should be left for each person. The back could again be 400–450 mm high. For comfort, cant the back of the bench about 15 degrees and lift the front of the seat about 5 degrees. This will also prevent water from lying on the seat.

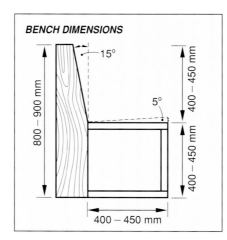

BENCH DIMENSIONS

15°
5°
800 – 900 mm
400 – 450 mm
400 – 450 mm
400 – 450 mm

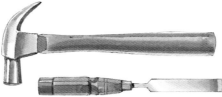

1 Taper off one corner of two 300 x 25 mm timbers and attach them to both sides of a post, nailing a short piece of 100 x 50 mm between them to support the leg assembly. Repeat for other supports. To prevent rust, use hot-dipped galvanised nails for outdoor projects.

3 For comfort, round off the front edges of the 100 x 50 mm seat and back slats with a plane or router. You can also buy pre-routed boards. For seating, use only good quality, splinterless timber, and seal it well. Careful finishing is important when making benches and other seats, as only a comfortable bench will be a useful addition to your outdoor furniture.

Hint
If you want to use a clear film on timber for outdoor structures, use a good quality marine varnish. Other types of clear lacquer don't handle an exterior environment well and you will often need to replace them.

2 For the legs, assemble three-sided 100 x 50 mm boxes. Slip these into the back support, and nail them to the cross-braces and deck. Also nail through the 300 x 25 mm pieces into the 100 x 50 mm boxes. Check that everything is plumb, level and square.

4 Nail back slats to each 300 x 25 mm piece. Nail seat slats to the 100 x 50 mm legs. Countersink nail heads so that they don't snag clothing. Cap the back with a 150 x 25 or 150 x 50 mm timber to protect cut ends from moisture that could cause rot. If you prefer, screw fix the slats for greater security, but be sure to use brass screws and countersink them below the surface.

A COMFY CORNER
This attractive and all-purpose bench is just the thing to make use of a spare corner of a deck or porch. It is simple to construct, and the size can be adjusted to suit most spaces. Do, however, keep in mind the standard bench dimensions given opposite.

Use 150 mm timber for the beam if you are spanning more than 1200 mm, and be sure to insert struts of 75 x 25 mm timbers at 400 mm centres. For the seating slats also you can use 75 x 25 mm timbers. Leave 5 mm spaces between them to allow water to drain away.

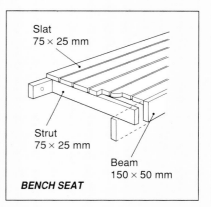

Slat
75 × 25 mm

Strut
75 × 25 mm

Beam
150 × 50 mm

BENCH SEAT

Use a router to round off the edges of the slats and then sandpaper them to remove splinters or rough bits that could catch at clothes (and skin!). Paint or stain the wood as desired.

This simple bench is just the way to fill in an awkward corner. Once it's there, you'll be surprised how often you use it.

MAKING SIMPLE BENCHES

A SECLUDED ALCOVE

You can make a private corner any-where with these comfortable but easy-to-build slatted seats. Bolt the verticals to the floor joists and then cantilever the seat from them.

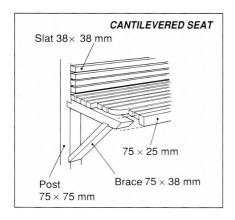

CANTILEVERED SEAT
Slat 38× 38 mm
75 × 25 mm
Post 75 × 75 mm
Brace 75 × 38 mm

A SIMPLE SHELF-SEAT

A simple bench will provide seating or a useful shelf on a ground-level deck. Bolt the 100 x 100 mm uprights to the floor joists and add two 75 x 25 mm cross-pieces at each end. Space the 150 x 38 mm slats slightly apart to allow water to drain off.

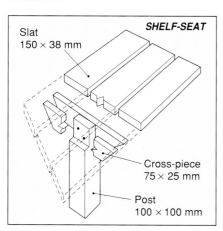

SHELF-SEAT
Slat 150 × 38 mm
Cross-piece 75 × 25 mm
Post 100 × 100 mm

These slatted seats leave the deck free as they are cantilevered. The built-in backs ensure comfort and provide some shelter from the wind.

This basic bench achieves an individual look as the ends are cut away diagonally to follow the lines of the deck edges.

IDEAL ENTERTAINING AREA

A firepit surrounded by benches is the ideal arrangement for an outdoor meal when the weather is becoming a little crisp.

A firepit and surrounding benches provide an ideal area for entertaining. To be safe, position the firepit well away from the house or trees—or replace it with a paved area for a portable barbecue. We added a timber floor but the arrangement will work equally well with grass or any paving.

The floor and benches are constructed from on-edge 100 x 50 mm timbers with internal spacers. Be sure to use cedar or treated pine for any members that come in contact with the ground.

1 Select and prepare a level site. Ensure the decking is raised above the ground (see page 32).

2 Lay out the deck to visualise the finished product.

3 Excavate the base area to 100–150 mm and fill the area with a level bed of sand or gravel.

4 Assemble a decking base of 100 x 100 mm timber. Skew nail the base pieces together.

5 Lay 100 x 50 mm decking boards on edge, nailing them together with 5 mm spacers between. Skew nail to the 100 x 100 mm members.

6 Dig post holes and set posts for bench supports (see diagram). Bolt cross-pieces to the tops of the posts and assemble the seats.

7 Stain the deck, or apply a transparent preservative.

8 Complete the project by lining the firepit with concrete block or stone.

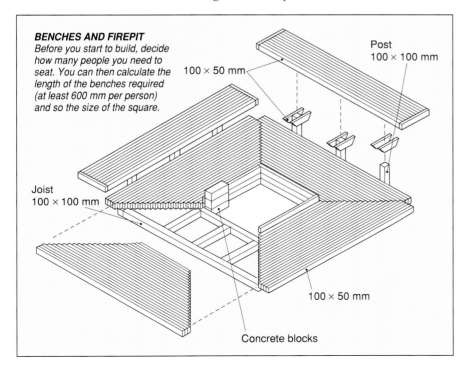

BENCHES AND FIREPIT
Before you start to build, decide how many people you need to seat. You can then calculate the length of the benches required (at least 600 mm per person) and so the size of the square.

100 × 50 mm

Post
100 × 100 mm

Joist
100 × 100 mm

100 × 50 mm

Concrete blocks

Mosaic table

This beautiful table will provide the finishing touch for your patio. It is simple to make—but test assemble the slats before you start building so that you can check the lengths are correct.

Geometric patterns of clear coated timber strips give an inlaid appearance to this attractive table. If you want, you can build matching benches. Just use construction techniques similar to those given for the table and see the information on bench basics on page 44.

The table measures approximately 1.2 x 0.9 m and is 425 mm high. It used 1.8 m of 75 x 75 mm, 8.5 m of 75 x 50 mm and 26 m of 50 x 25 mm dressed Western red cedar.

1 Glue and nail mitred 75 x 50 mm timbers (tabletop sides and ends) to form the tabletop frame.

2 Cut 75 x 75 mm uprights to size to form the legs. Screw one upright into each corner of the frame, countersinking the screw heads and then plugging the holes.

3 Install the 75 x 50 mm stretcher inside the frame. Strengthen with 75 x 50 mm side and diagonal cross-members, mitring corners wherever it is necessary.

4 Mitre corners on four 50 x 25 mm (edge slats) to form the outer frame of the tabletop. Cut the other 50 x 25 mm slats to size and, if desired, stain and varnish them.

5 Install the tabletop, starting with the outer 50 x 25 mm slats and working toward the centre. Glue and nail slats to the base, spacing them approximately 5 mm apart. Countersink the nail heads and fill the holes.

Hint
When using glue on outdoor structures, use epoxy resin as it won't break down when it rains. Follow the manufacturer's instructions carefully and don't mix too much together at one time.

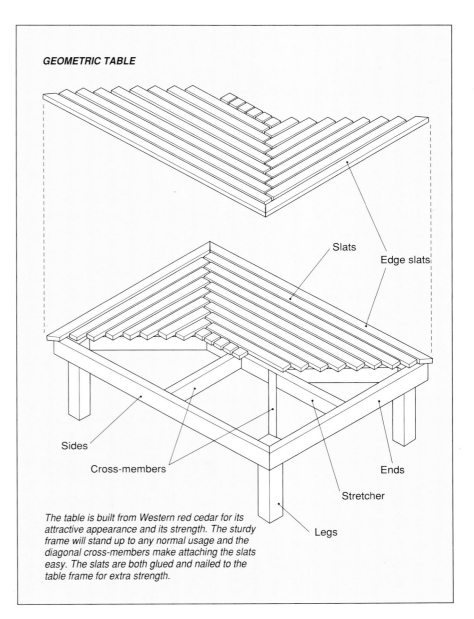

GEOMETRIC TABLE

Slats

Edge slats

Sides

Cross-members

Ends

Stretcher

Legs

The table is built from Western red cedar for its attractive appearance and its strength. The sturdy frame will stand up to any normal usage and the diagonal cross-members make attaching the slats easy. The slats are both glued and nailed to the table frame for extra strength.

MATERIALS LIST

Component	Material (DAR)	Length (mm)	No.
Legs	75 x 75	400	4
Tabletop sides	75 x 50	1180	2
Tabletop ends	75 x 50	890	2
Stretcher	75 x 50	1100	1
Cross-member (side)	75 x 50	385	2
Cross-member (diagonal)	75 x 50	510	4
Slats (side edge)	50 x 25	1200	2
Slats (end edge)	50 x 25	914	2
Slats	50 x 25		

Other: Wood plugs, glue, screws, nails, wood putty, stain (if required), varnish

Picnic Setting

This picnic table and benches have been designed to be simple to build and fun to use. Made from fine sawn oregon or cedar, they will provide a perfect setting for your outdoor entertaining. Make three benches to provide seating for six.

TABLE

1 Mark the halfway point on two of the three spokes and draw parallel lines at 60 degrees from the edge and 100 mm apart. Repeat these in the opposite direction to form two crosses. Cut along the lines with a tenon saw to leave the pointed housing to a depth of 34 mm. Chisel out centres.

2 On the third spoke, mark the halfway point and draw parallel lines as before. Cut along one set of parallel lines on one side and the second set on the other so that the cuts go in opposite directions. Cut each side to a depth of 17 mm only.

3 Slot the central joint together, as shown in the diagram, checking that all the radial angles are 60 degrees, and then drill, glue and bolt the joint together.

4 Saw the ends of each spoke so that, from the midpoint, one end is 700 mm long with square ends and the other end is 725 mm long with 120 degree points.

5 Place the square ends of the spokes flush on top of the legs and nail them in position with connecting plates fixed so that they rise 50 mm above the leg and flush with the spoke (see diagram detail). Use 60 mm nails to fix the plates to the outside and the edges of the legs, and into the spokes. Nail through the spokes into the top of the legs with 75 mm nails.

6 Fit the three braces between the legs by mitring the ends at 60 degrees and cutting a 100 x 50 mm housing in the centre of each to take the spokes.

7 Cut the ends of the table top slats at 60 degrees (their diagonal length at the spoke will be 110 mm). Mark out their positions with 10 mm gaps between each round and use 75 mm nails to fix them in place on the spokes, completing one full circuit at a time. You may need to trim the spokes to fit.

This hexagonal table and matching seats are just right for picnic meals in the garden—and they're fast and easy to make.

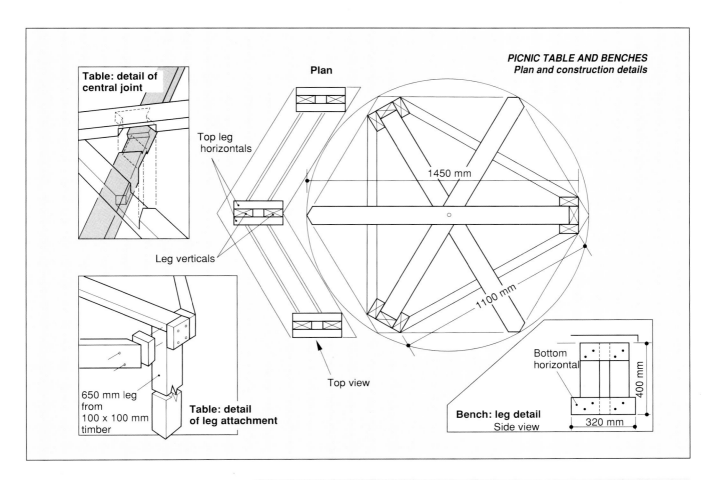

Table: detail of central joint

Plan

Top leg horizontals

Leg verticals

1450 mm

1100 mm

Top view

650 mm leg from 100 x 100 mm timber

Table: detail of leg attachment

Bottom horizontal

400 mm

Bench: leg detail
Side view

320 mm

BENCH

1 Construct the leg structure. Each leg requires two 400 mm verticals, two 260 mm horizontals for the top and one 320 mm horizontal for the leg bottom.

2 As the angle at the centre of the bench is 120 degrees, cut all the ends of the seat slats at 60 degrees and parallel to each other.

3 Lay the slats out upside down and nail the legs to them. Then turn the seat over and nail it from the top.

4 Saw the ends of the top horizontals along the same angle as the seat slats.

Hint

Whenever you are using timber, make sure all your cutting tools are very sharp before you begin work. Sharp tools not only make your work easier, they allow your cuts to be more precise.

MATERIALS LIST

	Material (mm)	Length/size (mm)	Quantity
Table			
Spokes	100 x 50	1500	3
Legs	100 x 100	650	3
Braces	100 x 50	1100	3
Connecting plates	100 x 25	100	3
		125	6
Slats	100 x 50	800	6
		675	6
		550	6
		425	6
		300	6
		175	6
Bench (Makes 1)			
Leg verticals	100 x 50	400	6
Leg horizontals	100 x 50	260	6
		320	3
Slats	100 x 50	850	6

Other: One 65 mm long bolt and nut; 60 mm nails; 75 mm nails; glue

MAKING A TREE SEAT

This hexagonal seat will be the perfect spot to relax on a summer afternoon. Build it around your favourite tree, even if it is still a sapling. Just be sure the fully grown trunk will fit within the 600 mm central gap. If the trunk is, or will become, larger than that, you will need to enlarge the circle of the seat and cut the slats longer.

1 Establish the position of the bench. Working from the tree, mark out two equilateral triangles with 1575 mm sides to form a star with six points. The correct angle at each corner will be 60°. The opposite pairs of points will be 1850 mm apart: these points are where the front edge of each of the six supports will rest at ground level (marked 'Check point' on the diagram opposite).

2 Cut the support components (see Materials list). Use a jigsaw to shape curves on the cross-support and rear support (for the seat).

3 Assemble the six support frames. Use 175 mm bolts to attach two cross-supports to each rear and front support and coach screws to fix the bottom ends of the front and rear supports to each other.

4 Dig 400 mm deep holes at the six points of the marked-out star. Creosote the lower portions of the supports and stand them in the holes so that the check points are at

the points of the star. Use lengths of scrap timber to prop the supports in position, nailing them as necessary.

5 Lay a length of timber to one side of the tree trunk and check that each pair of supports is parallel and an equal distance from the trunk. Use a spirit level to check the vertical angle and the horizontal angle of the seat.

6 Fill the six holes with concrete and allow at least 24 hours before removing the props.

7 Measure between the supports as placed and make any necessary adjustments to slat lengths. Then

cut slats to size. Lay test strips of slats across from one back and seat support to another and use a sliding bevel measuring from the centre line of each frame, and tenon saw to assess and cut the angle.

8 Fit the front seat slats and top back slats all round first, mitring the ends to the correct angle as you go. These will brace the whole structure. Now space the remaining slats evenly as shown in the diagram, bevelling edges where it may be necessary.

9 Finish the seat with paint or varnish as desired.

A tree seat is a practical addition to a garden, providing seating in the shade without taking up too much room. It adds a romantic touch, too.

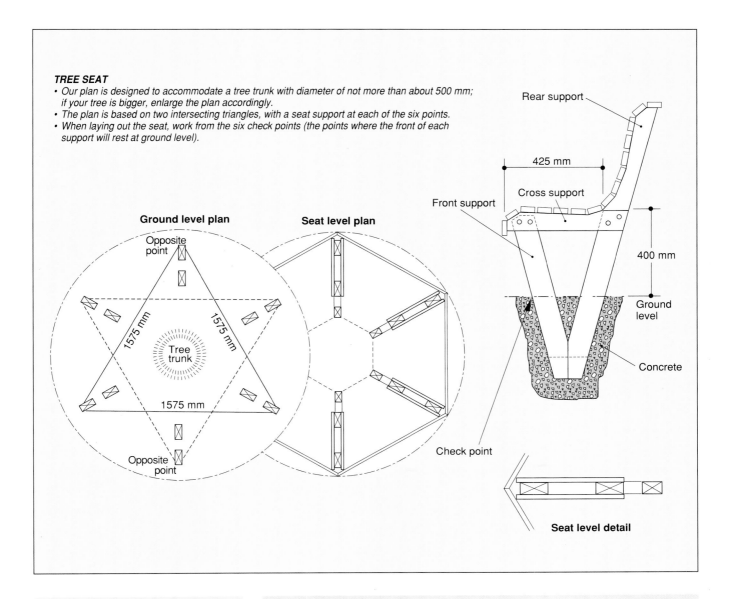

TREE SEAT
- *Our plan is designed to accommodate a tree trunk with diameter of not more than about 500 mm; if your tree is bigger, enlarge the plan accordingly.*
- *The plan is based on two intersecting triangles, with a seat support at each of the six points.*
- *When laying out the seat, work from the six check points (the points where the front of each support will rest at ground level).*

Ground level plan

Opposite point

1575 mm

1575 mm

1575 mm

Tree trunk

Opposite point

Seat level plan

Seat level detail

Rear support

425 mm

Cross support

Front support

400 mm

Ground level

Concrete

Check point

USING ELECTRIC SAWS
- Hold the work with clamps.
- Always keep two hands on the saw and feet on the ground.
- Unplug the saw if adjusting it.
- Set the saw depth to cut a fraction more than the timber thickness.
- Support the work so that it won't jam the saw blade.
- Never stand behind the saw in case it throws back at you.
- Keep the work area clean so there is nothing to trip on.
- Make sure the lead is well clear of the blade at all times.
- Never immobilise or remove the telescoping guard.

MATERIALS LIST

Component	Material (mm)	Length or size (mm)	Quantity
Front supports	100 x 50 green hardwood	750	6
Rear supports	100 x 50 green hardwood	1300	6
Cross supports	100 x 50 oregon	525	12
Seat slats	50 x 25 oregon	1020	12
		1010	6
		1000	6
		950	6
		850	6
		750	6
Back slats	50 x 25 oregon	600	48

Other: Twenty-four 175 x 10 mm cuphead bolts, nuts and washers; six 100 mm coach screws; 50 mm galvanised bullet-head nails; two bags sand and cement; creosote; paint or varnish to finish

WINDOW BOXES

The most convenient way to fix a window box in place is to use a wide sill but if you don't have one, fit brackets to the wall. Be sure the brackets are firmly fixed, as a window box filled with soil will be extremely heavy.

Wet soil will rot any timber, so a window box with no base is preferable. Use long polystyrene foam or plastic planters as liners—this will also make it easier when replanting as the entire planter can be removed. Planters come in a variety of sizes and may or may not have a top lip that can rest on a batten. Those without a lip, including foam planters, are better supported underneath with a slatted or strutted floor. You may find it easier to buy the planter first and construct a window box to suit.

Make the framework from 38 x 25 mm oregon or treated pine. The front and ends can be made from oregon, Western red cedar or other timber. For a rustic look use rough sawn timbers.

A BASIC BOX

1 Calculate the dimensions required for the window box, paying particular attention to the width: if the liner is to rest on the battens, they should be the same distance apart as the width of the planter just below the lip (see above right).

2 Make a framework of 38 x 25 mm timbers. Insert struts in front,

A window box gives the finishing touch to a house and is easy to make—even someone with no woodworking experience will be able to build one.

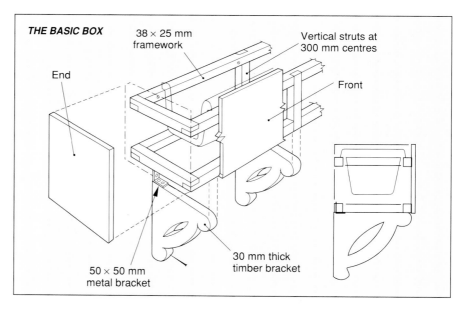

THE BASIC BOX
38 × 25 mm framework
Vertical struts at 300 mm centres
End
Front
50 × 50 mm metal bracket
30 mm thick timber bracket

back and along the bottom at 300 mm centres; if you are using more than one liner placed end to end within the box, also include horizontal struts at the top for them to rest on.

3 Fix brackets to the wall at approximately 600 mm centres, using coach screws that should penetrate 75 mm into the timber frame of the wall. For masonry walls use expanding masonry bolts that penetrate approximately 50 mm into the wall. Use 30 mm thick plain or decorative timber brackets or pressed steel angle brackets.

4 Place the frame on the brackets and fix it securely to them. If using timber brackets, fix the window box to them with 50 x 50 mm metal brackets (see diagram).

5 Fix the front and end boards (about 16 mm thick) to the box. They should extend above the battens or top frame to conceal the top edge of the liner.

ADD A SLATTED BASE

This window box (right) is made using the same steps as the basic box, but a floor of spaced 41 x 19 mm slats has been added. The solid timber brackets are fitted to the wall with dowels and the frame is fixed to the wall with screws for added strength. An exterior top trim of 41 x 19 mm timber gives a neat finish.

A TAPERED BOX

Instead of a frame, this box (below) consists of solid front, back and ends. The floor of 41 x 19 mm slats rests on cleats fixed to the end boards and on the solid timber brackets. Use 75 mm x 10 g screws (and plastic plugs for masonry walls) to fix the brackets and back to the wall. The end boards have been tapered to give a sloping front.

Tapered ends give a neat finish to this elegant window box.

This simple box has a slatted base for drainage and a trim around the top to emphasise the shape. It is supported on solid timber brackets.

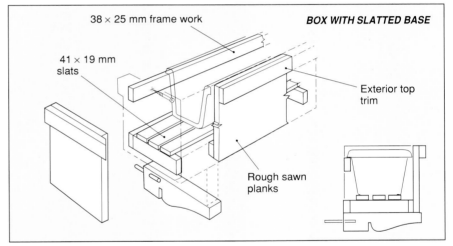

BOX WITH SLATTED BASE

38 x 25 mm frame work

41 x 19 mm slats

Exterior top trim

Rough sawn planks

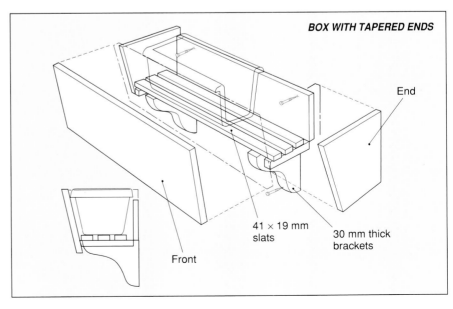

BOX WITH TAPERED ENDS

End

41 x 19 mm slats

30 mm thick brackets

Front

LETTERBOX

This smart and easy-to-make letterbox will add distinction to your house. The solid post is finished with an ornamental knob and supports an arm on which the box itself sits. The box contains a slot for letters and, above it, a space for newspaper and other large articles. The circular opening to this space is framed with a brass circle and you can add brass house numbers to the plaque that hangs from the arm. Never again will anyone have difficulty identifying your house!

We chose Western red cedar for our letterbox as it stands up to the elements so well, but treated pine is a cheaper substitute that will still look attractive. Buy the knob for the top of the post from your local wood turner; the brass ring for the newspaper hole can be purchased at a hardware store (or have it made to size by a sheet-metal worker).

THE LETTERBOX

1 Mark out the individual pieces on the stock, using a combination square, pencil and tape, and leaving spaces (at least 5 mm) for saw cuts. Cut out each piece, cutting on the waste side of each line and planing them to size: the base (330 x 230 x 19 mm), two sides (each 300 x 230 x 19 mm), the bottom front (162 x 50 x 19 mm), top front (180 x 162

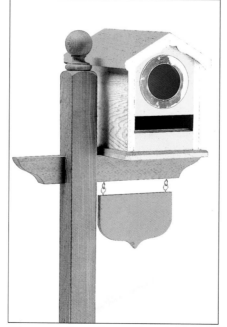

The same letterbox painted four different ways. The design adapts well to modern or heritage style—just choose colours to complement your house.

x 19 mm), back (162 x 90 x 19 mm), door flap (160 x 88 x 19 mm), shelf (281 x 162 x 19 mm) and two roof pieces (340 x 145 x 19 mm). When planing the end grain, plane from the edges to the centre to avoid chipping out.

2 Place all pieces that are to finish the same width in a vice and plane them to the same width.

3 Place the top front and back together, mark the centre point on the top edge and then 45 mm down from the top on each side (the shape of the gable). Place the top front and back together in a vice and cut away the corners, finally planing them both to shape (always plane towards the apex).

4 To make the newspaper hole in the top front, mark a point in the centre, about 80 mm up from the bottom. From it, use a compass to draw a circle 90 mm in diameter. Drill an 8 mm hole in the centre of the circle to begin the cut and then use an electric jigsaw or a coping saw to cut the hole. Sand the edge.

5 Take the bottom front and plane an outward bevel along the top edge. (This should prevent rain water entering the mail slot.)

6 Bevel the lower edge of the door inwards and round the top edge slightly. Make a 12 mm diameter hole in the centre, near the bottom edge, so that the flap will be able to be opened.

7 Bevel and plane the long edges of the roof pieces so that they fit together neatly on the gables. If possible, use a sliding bevel to determine the angle. The roof projects about 20 mm beyond the gables.

8 Bevel or chamfer the edges of the base to provide a neat finish.

9 Test assemble the pieces and mark the position of the side walls on the base. Place one side wall in a vice upside down, spread epoxy resin adhesive on the edge and position the base on it. Nail home using 40 mm nails. Repeat the process with the other side.

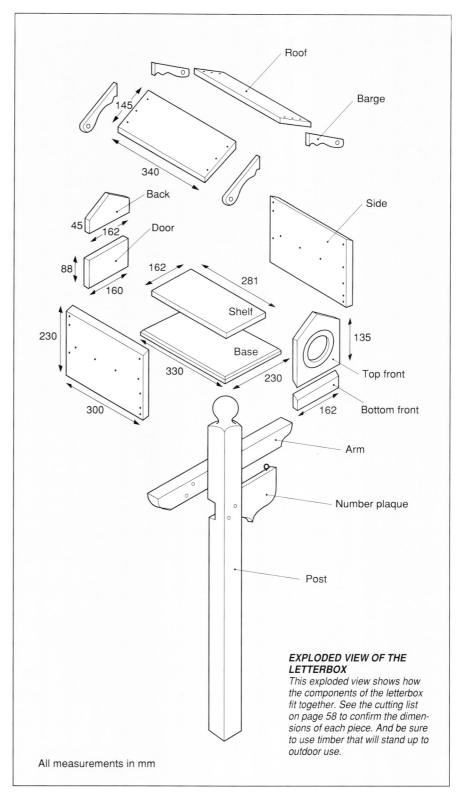

EXPLODED VIEW OF THE LETTERBOX
This exploded view shows how the components of the letterbox fit together. See the cutting list on page 58 to confirm the dimensions of each piece. And be sure to use timber that will stand up to outdoor use.

All measurements in mm

10 Glue and align the bottom front between the sides and nail in position. Repeat for the gable pieces. Apply adhesive to the front and side edges of the shelf and slide it into position. Fix with nails. Leave overnight to dry.

11 Plane the top edges of the sides so that they slope down, continuing the line of the gables. Apply epoxy resin adhesive to the gable tops and fix down one roof piece. Then repeat the fixing process for the other roof piece.

12 Using a combination square, mark on each side a point 12 mm down from the shelf and 10 mm in from the edge for the door pivots. Plane the door to fit the opening (allowing 1 mm all around). Wedge it into position using a piece of cardboard and drive 40 mm bullet-head nails through the marked pivot positions into the door. The door should swing freely. On the base, glue and nail a door stop (a small, flat piece of timber) into position to prevent the door swinging inwards.

13 If desired, now make the barge pieces for front and back. Make a cardboard template to the required shape and then cut the pieces from 6 mm Western red cedar.

THE POST AND SUPPORT

1 Using 75 x 75 mm timber, cut a post 1500 mm long and the arm 500 mm long.

2 Mark out housing joints 300 mm from the top of the post and 334 mm from one end of the arm. Cut both to a depth of 30 mm.

3 Shape the ends of the arm.

4 Lightly chamfer all edges, place arm and post together and drill them to receive two 75 x 6 mm cuphead galvanised bolts. Use washers behind the nuts.

5 Centre the letterbox near the post on the longer projecting arm and from the underside, use a pencil to mark the position of two bolts on both sides of the arm and the base of the letterbox, 50 mm in from the sides of the letterbox. Drill 6.5 mm diameter holes through the arm and the base of the letterbox. Enlarge the hole in the base of the arm (using a drill or chisel) to 24 mm diameter to a depth of 15 mm, to take the nut. Insert two 75 x 6 mm cuphead bolts from the inside of the letterbox and tighten using a socket spanner. Don't forget to add the washers.

6 Cut and shape the number plaque from Western red cedar and fix it

to the arm using brassplated hooks and eyes. Use pliers to close the hook around the eye to prevent it coming off.

7 Fix a turned knob to the top of the post, using dowel. Varnish or paint the structure as required. Finally, screw the brass ring to the newspaper ring and house numbers to the plaque.

8 Unscrew the letterbox and number plate from the arm. Select a prominent and easily accessible position for your structure and dig a hole 150 x 150 mm and 300 mm deep. Prepare concrete (half a bucket of sand/cement mix) and place it in the hole. Insert the post in the

cement mix and prop it up so that it is vertical and level. Leave for two days and then reassemble the letterbox and number plate.

MATERIALS LIST

1200 mm of 250 x 25 mm Western red cedar (for base, sides), 1800 mm of 175 x 25 mm Western red cedar (for front, back, door, shelf, roof), 2100 mm of 75 x 75 mm Western red cedar (for post and arm), four 75 x 6 mm cuphead galvanised bolts, 40 mm bullet-head nails, 65 mm turned knob, 130 mm diameter brass face plate with 90 mm central hole, brass house numbers, epoxy resin adhesive.

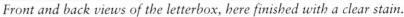
Front and back views of the letterbox, here finished with a clear stain.

CUTTING LIST

Component	Length (mm)	Width (mm)	Th. (mm)	Quantity
Post	1500	66	66	1
Arm	500	66	30	1
Base	330	230	19	1
Sides	300	230	19	2
Shelf	281	162	19	1
Top front	180	162	19	1
Bottom front	162	50	19	1
Door	160	88	19	1
Back	162	90	19	1
Roof	340	145	19	2
Barges	145	40	6	4
No. plaque	200	150	19	1

MULTI-PURPOSE GARDEN BOX

These simple-to-make multi-purpose boxes can be made to any size and used for planters, seating or tables. Our planter is an 800 mm cube and we chose 500 mm as a good bench/seat height.

1 Make the frames from rough sawn 75 x 75 mm and 75 x 38 mm oregon. Use half-lap joints at the top plate corners and at every 350 mm include a side stud to which you can nail the cladding.

2 Nail dressed Western red cedar tongue and groove boards to the sides and the tops of table and bench boxes.

3 Add 25 x 12 mm bottom and corner trims for a neat finish.

4 Use a clear exterior oil finish and your multi-purpose boxes will last indefinitely outside.

MATERIALS LIST FOR PLANTER

Component	Size (mm)	Length (mm)	Quantity
Frame upright	75 x 75	800	4
Frame top/bottom	75 x 38	800	8
Studs	75 x 38	800	4
Cladding	175 x 15	800	20
Trims	25 x 12	800	8
Top trim	100 x 19	800	4

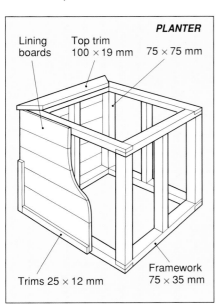

PLANTER

Lining boards
Top trim 100 × 19 mm
75 × 75 mm
Trims 25 × 12 mm
Framework 75 × 35 mm

The basic pattern for the planter can be adapted to make a bench or table by omitting the top trim and adding a slightly projecting top.

BIRD FEEDER

Birds will flock to your garden when you hang this practical and attractive bird feeder from a large tree or pergola (but be sure it is out of reach of neighbourhood cats). Made from Western red cedar, it will stand up to the elements, and the ramin dowels used for the perches are strong enough to withstand the claws of most birds. If you intend to feed cockatoos and rosellas, however, you will need to use even sturdier timbers and modify the measurements to make the bird feeder larger.

We used a lathe to shape the posts for design interest but you may use squared posts for a simpler structure. Your local wood turner could produce shaped posts to fit or may even have small posts in stock. The style will adapt well to most situations, from heritage to modern.

1 Cut the base (slightly oversize) from 250 x 25 mm Western red cedar, and then plane it to 350 x 230 x 19 mm. Cut the two gables, ridge and two roof pieces from 175 x 19 mm Western red cedar and plane to the appropriate sizes: each gable 235 x 60 x 15, the ridge 390 x 50 x 15 and the roof pieces each 350 x 160 x 15 mm. When planing, work from each end towards the centre to prevent any breaking out of the fibres.

2 On one gable, mark the centre point on one long side and then draw lines from that point to the opposite corners so as to form a triangle 235 x 130 x 130. Place both gables together in a vice and plane (or carefully cut) the gables to shape, working from the centre (apex) of the gable to the ends.

3 Take the ridge and cut out 47 mm from each end to a depth of 30 mm (see detail on diagram). If desired, use a coping saw to cut out a decorative shape on the 20 mm at each end of the ridge.

4 Cut four posts 200 mm long from 19 x 19 mm Western red cedar. In one end of each post drill a hole 9.5 mm in diameter and 15 mm deep for the dowel that will fix the post to the bottom (use an off-cut from the perch dowel). Also drill a hole 5 mm deep and centred in one side 30 mm from the bottom, to receive the 9.5 mm diameter perch. At the other end of each post, cut out a rebate 15 x 9.5 mm (see diagram) in the opposite side from the perch hole. If desired, now round or shape the posts, using either a lathe, plane or spoke shave.

5 On the base, use a combination square rule to mark two sides of the post positions, each 18 mm in from the edge. Use pencil as pen is hard to sand off. Number each post position and corresponding post. Stand each post in position on the base and mark the position of the other two sides. Find the centre point within each post position and drill a hole, 9.5 mm in diameter and 10 mm deep, to take the dowel. If desired, now shape the edges of the base, using a router or chamfer with a plane.

6 Centre the gables against the short sides of the base and transfer the inside post marks to the gables. Lay the gables down, place the correct post to the outside of each mark and mark the thickness of the posts on the gable (this gives the width of the housing).

Made from stained Western red cedar, this bird feeder is truly elegant but it would be just as smart if brightly painted to suit more flamboyant tastes.

7 Use your square to complete marking out of the housings on the gable ends and cut the housings the full height of the gables and to a depth of 3 mm.

8 Cut the perches from 9.5 mm diameter ramin dowel (two 282 mm long and two 150 mm).

9 Take the gables and flatten about 10 mm off the apex so that the ridge sits flat down on them. Take the roof pieces and bevel the long sides so that they sit on the gables and against the ridge. Use a sliding bevel if you have one and make sure the edges remain parallel.

10 Test assemble the pieces without using glue to ensure all pieces fit accurately and plumb. Make any necessary adjustments.

11 Place the ridge piece vertically in a vice, and then glue and nail the gable ends to it. Check that the gable ends are parallel to each other and square with the ridge.

12 Glue and nail the roof pieces to the gable ends. Remember to line them up evenly and avoid nailing into the post housings. Leave overnight to dry.

13 Apply glue to the gable housings and posts and place them together. If they do not fit snugly, use 15 mm panel pins to secure the joints from inside the roof space.

14 Use a pencil end or trimmed dowel to apply glue to the perch holes and the dowel holes in the posts. (Be careful not to use too much glue.) Insert the perch pieces and the dowels.

15 Apply glue to the dowel holes in the base and insert the post structure. Ensure that all posts are plumb and parallel, and if possible apply a light cramp pressure between perch pieces and base to ensure good joints. Leave overnight to dry.

16 Cut the stop rails to go between the posts from Western red cedar: two 270 x 15 x 12 mm and two 140 x 15 x 12 mm. Sand them back, chamfering the top edge. Apply a small bead of glue to the

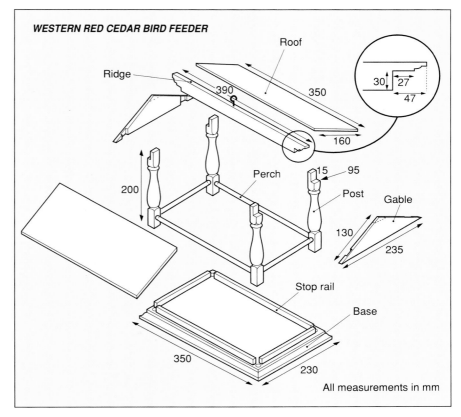

WESTERN RED CEDAR BIRD FEEDER

Roof — Ridge — 390 — 350 — 30 27 47 — 160 — 200 — Perch — 15 95 — Post — Gable — 130 — 235 — Stop rail — Base — 350 — 230 — All measurements in mm

bottom of the rails and press them into place.

17 Find the centre of the ridge and use a bradawl or 3 mm drill to make a pilot hole for the hook or eye that will be used to hold the feeder up. It will be even more stable if you use a hook and eye at each end of the ridge. If desired, put a hook on the inside to hold a solid birdseed bell.

18 Sand the finished bird feeder. You may then coat it with good quality teak oil or raw linseed oil to preserve the timber, or apply an exterior acrylic paint in colours to suit your taste.

MATERIALS LIST

One 900 mm length of 250 x 25 mm Western red cedar, one 600 mm length of 175 x 19 mm Western red cedar, 1 m length of 9.5 mm diameter ramin dowel, suspension hook, nails, 15 mm panel pins, epoxy resin adhesive.

CUTTING LIST

Component	Length (mm)	Width (mm)	Th. (mm)	Quantity
Base	350	230	19	1
Gable	235	65	15	2
Ridge	390	50	15	1
Roof	350	160	15	2
Post	200	19	19	4
Stop rail	270	15	12	2
Stop rail	140	15	12	2
Perch	282	9.5 dia.		2
Perch	150	9.5 dia.		2

SIMPLE BARBECUE

A good barbecue is basic to the enjoyment of outdoor living. It should be located within easy reach of the kitchen and a shady outdoor eating area, but away from foliage that could catch fire.

You don't need to be an expert to build a simple barbecue, just remember to plan it carefully and to check constantly for horizontal and vertical levels. We used a curved back wall for extra interest, but you can follow the same steps to make a squared design.

PLANNING YOUR BARBECUE

Choose the bricks carefully. A barbecue is a small structure and so bricks without a lot of contrasting markings are most suitable. The bricks shown here are PGH Bounty sandstock bricks.

Plan the size of the barbecue on paper. This one was planned around a prefabricated hotplate and grate (from Barbeques Galore). It comes with its own supporting angle-iron frame. The unit measures 660 x 480 mm and you will have to allow 225 mm of brickwork outside that. We had to make some of the mortar joints as wide as 15 mm in order to expand the structure sufficiently to fit the hotplate unit. Adding one cap of plaster sizer or washing up detergent makes mortar more workable.

This simple barbecue can be made with a round or square back, but whichever style you choose it will still cook to perfection.

1 Lay out the area and dig it out to a depth of one brick. Set common bricks into a mortar bed. For the mortar use 5 parts white bush sand and 1 part off-white cement.

2 Cover the foundation course with mortar and smooth over. Add water to make the bonding of the mortar with the next layer of bricks stronger.

3 Cut bricks if your design has a curved back. Use a cold chisel on grass or a brickie's bolster. This is more work, but worth it.

4 Using quality bricks, set out the first course as shown, filling wedge-shaped joints with mortar. Scrape joints off flush with bricks.

5 Check for level with a spirit level as you proceed. It is important to keep the courses level right from the beginning.

6 Continue upwards until there are seven courses, laying bricks over joints. Avoid running joints, as they will result in a weaker structure, liable to collapse.

7 Fill the centre with rubble or common bricks and concrete (4 parts washed river sand and gravel and 1 part ordinary cement is adequate) to make the fire platform.

8 Smooth the platform. Lay two courses of double thickness brickwork around the edge of the platform, checking regularly that the iron frame will fit.

9 Ensure that the bricks on the inside of the curve of these two courses are neatly cut as they will be visible behind the fire.

10 Lay mortar for a third course, setting into the mortar 75 mm lengths of 6 mm flat steel to take the frame.

11 Finish with a row of header bricks to trim and strengthen the structure. Your barbecue is now ready to enjoy.

MATERIALS LIST

300 quality bricks, 70 commons bricks, white bush sand, off-white cement, one container of plaster sizer, hotplate, grate, angle-iron frame, four lengths of 25 x 6 mm flat steel 75 mm long, rubble and cement for infill.

COMPLETE BARBECUE SETTING

This well-designed barbecue setting includes a handy plate rack, large storage cupboard and generous worktop. You will be well set up for your best barbecue ever.

The barbecue is built from bricks, with a concrete footing and steel bars for the grid. Don't cut the bars to fit until after you've built the barbecue, so you can be sure they'll fit. The cupboard has a timber frame and doors and the worktop is tiled for ease of use and cleaning. If you prefer, substitute 12 mm form ply for compressed cement for the worktop.

An attractive addition to any garden, this barbecue setting is big enough for any party of family or friends. It is also easy to use, with the built-in storage cupboard and tiled worktop.

1 Use pegs and string to peg out the site to 2200 x 760 mm and dig the area free of grass. Check that the site is level and dig out or fill if necessary.

2 Prepare premixed mortar, or mix 1 part cement, 1 part lime and 6 parts sand. Add one cap of plaster sizer or washing up detergent to make it easier to work.

3 Lay the first course in a mortar bed and tap to achieve a level. Use one row of bricks around the outline and one for the partition between fire and cupboard.

4 Run strip wire reinforcement mesh under the next course. Check for level. The wire reinforcement is an important part of the structure as it bonds the structure into a single block of masonry.

5 Stagger each course so that each brick is above a joint. Where necessary, cut bricks with a wide cold chisel or brickie's bolster and block hammer, placing them on a grass or sand bed.

6 Use wall ties at the junction points every third course to help bond the structure together. Lay only two courses for the front wall of the cupboard and five for the front of the fireplace.

7 As you go, build up corners a couple of courses, so you can use the L-shaped corner blocks to keep the courses straight. Put a screw in the top of the block to hold a string guideline in place.

8 Add another strip of wire reinforcement mesh above the mortar on top of the seventh course of bricks. Lay an eighth course of bricks, then another mortar course on top. Smooth the mortar.

9 Set four 100 mm long flat steel supports on top of the eighth course. Place them across the wall so that they project inwards. They will support the notched angle iron for the grill.

10 On the tenth course place bricks cross-wise across end walls and partition to form projections. Include wall ties above the partition's projecting course.

11 Lay two more courses of bricks in normal staggered bond along back and part way along end walls and partition. Include two flat steel plate-warmer supports between the courses (see diagram). Add one more brick course along back.

12 Fill in the bottom of the cupboard and fireplace with bricks and mortar. Drill and bolt the angle iron plate rack to the flat steel supports. Position the notched angle iron and bars. You have now completed the basic structure of your new barbecue setting.

MATERIALS LIST

250 exterior bricks, 40 commons bricks, two bags mortar, one roll 90 mm wide mesh reinforcement, three wall ties, six 100 mm lengths of 25 mm flat steel, two 590 mm lengths and a 960 mm length of 38 mm angle iron, six 8 x 25 mm bolts, nuts and washers, nine approx. 960 mm long 12 mm mild steel bars, 3 m of 50 x 25 mm Western red cedar, 3 m of 25 x 25 mm Western red cedar, 1500 x 900 mm sheet of 15 mm compressed cement *or* 900 x 600 mm of 12 mm form ply, 7.5 m of cedar lining boards, two door knobs, four 100 mm T-hinges, 1 m² tiles.

THE CUPBOARD AND WORKTOP

Let the brickwork sit until the mortar is completely dry. You can then begin work on the cupboard and worktop. Make the door frame by fitting together a 50 x 25 mm frame and then nailing 25 x 25 mm timber along the rear edge of the 50 x 25s. Cut the 25 x 25 mm timber to enable the joints to interlock (see the picture for step 3).

To finish, add an extra lining board across the front of the tiles, above the door.

1 Sit the door frame in place to check that it will sit square within the brick opening.

5 Butt join 50 x 50 mm timbers to make the frame for the worktop. Place it in position to check fit and then nail home.

6 Drill holes into the brickwork and screw the frame in place so that it rests on the door frame. Check for level as you go.

7 Cut compressed cement to fit the top frame, and screw it in place. Plan the number of tiles that will fit across the worktop. Cut tiles to fit.

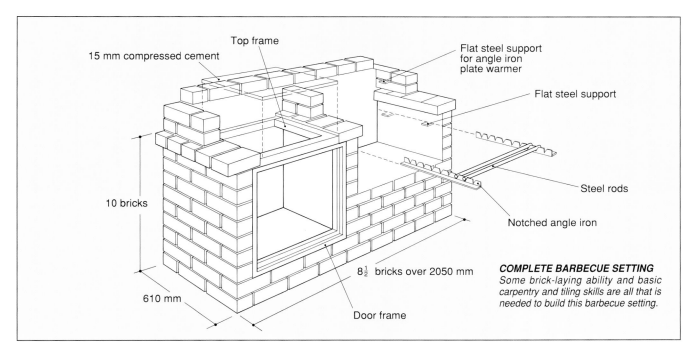

15 mm compressed cement

Top frame

Flat steel support for angle iron plate warmer

Flat steel support

Steel rods

Notched angle iron

10 bricks

610 mm

8½ bricks over 2050 mm

Door frame

COMPLETE BARBECUE SETTING
Some brick-laying ability and basic carpentry and tiling skills are all that is needed to build this barbecue setting.

2 Check that the top horizontal sits perfectly level, or the worktop will slope.

3 Nail the frame together, and then drill, plug and screw it in place. Check for square.

4 Make two doors using cedar lining boards and diagonal braces across the back. Ensure they fit.

8 Start tiling at the front, laying tiles on a 10 mm bed of mortar against a flat edge. Wet tiles to help the bonding process.

9 Cut tiles to fit at back and sides. Use a straight edge, spirit level and block or mallet to tap the tile surface flat.

10 Use mortar as grouting and to finish edges. Clean the tiles thoroughly before the mortar dries on them.

FENCES AND SCREENS

In an ideal world, fences wouldn't be necessary. We would be able to live secure in the knowledge that the rest of the world wouldn't trespass on our garden or even look in. But our world isn't ideal and whatever other structures you have in your garden, chances are you'll have, or want, a fence around it.

If your fence is too low for privacy and too nasty to bear looking at, take heart: there are many ways to improve it, and among our projects you'll find ideas that look good enough to feature as screens within the garden itself. We'll take a look at walls, too.

Many local councils have strong ideas about front fences, and it is a good idea to consult them before erecting any fence or wall. Fences on shared boundaries are a joint responsibility, and you'll need to come to an agreement with your neighbour about height, style and sharing the cost—but don't allow it to spark a neighbourhood feud!

If privacy is not a consideration and you need a fence only to prevent people and animals wandering in, a picket fence is ideal. The characteristic appearance is particularly suited to a cottage garden.

The front gate is the first impression most people get of a house, and so it should be welcoming as well as providing adequate security. This pergola gateway may be too elaborate for many, but it is certainly impressive.

BUILDING RETAINING WALLS

Check with your local building department before you start to build a retaining wall as you may need permission. Walls more than about a metre high are best left to professionals, but you can often avoid calling them in by terracing a steep slope with two or more low retaining walls.

Water is the worst enemy of a retaining wall. Without proper drainage, water will soon cause any structure you put up to buckle. In colder areas, alternating freeze–thaw cycles can also wreak havoc on a retaining wall. There are many different drainage systems you can use, the easiest being to leave open perpendicular joints every five or six joints in a masonry wall so that water can drain out, or to make weep holes by drilling them in timber or inserting short lengths of pipe through a wall near its base. You can also provide drainage by burying a PVC pipe behind the wall. Perforate the pipe so that water drains into it and ensure it extends well beyond the end of the wall. Slope the pipe at least 3 mm per 300 mm. With proper drainage, your wall should be strong.

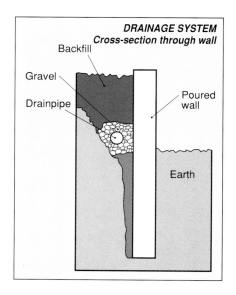

A plain concrete retaining wall may need to be dressed up with a plant or two but it is strong and long-lasting. Concrete is also relatively cheap, especially important if your wall is long.

CONCRETE RETAINING WALL

1 Dig a trench about 150–200 mm deep into the slope (in alpine areas it should be dug to a depth that is just below the frost line). Make the trench wide enough for the wall, with enough space for you to work in. You will need to build the formwork in it.

2 Cut 19 mm plywood into panels 90 mm taller than the height your wall will extend above the ground (earth provides the form for the footing). Coat plywood with motor oil for easier removal. Nail studs of 100 x 50 mm timber to the plywood, 600 mm apart.

3 Assemble the form with end pieces of plywood and interior spreaders of 100 x 50 mm wood. Set the form in place, make sure it is level and plumb, then brace it with outriggers and stakes. Push the form into place with one foot while you drive in the stakes.

4 To strengthen the wall, drive lengths of reinforcing rod into the ground every 450 mm. Tie reinforcing rods to the spreaders with wire. Tie horizontal reinforcing rods to the vertical ones every 450 mm. If you plan to cap the wall with concrete, let the vertical reinforcing rods protrude 25 mm or so above the spreaders' bottom edges.

5 Pour the concrete. This can be a big job, and you will need to be well prepared. Think out the process carefully and have a helper. We built a wheelbarrow ramp to the top of the form. As you pour, have a helper tamp the concrete to squeeze out air bubbles. After the concrete has set slightly, smooth its surface with a float and leave it to cure.

6 After the concrete cures, remove the forms, install perforated drainpipe by laying it in a bed of gravel as shown in the diagram on page 70, then backfill. Cap the wall with brick, wood or precast concrete coping, if desired. Use the terrace created by the wall as a garden or cover with lawn or paving for recreational use.

MIXING CONCRETE

When mixing concrete by hand, there are three things to watch out for if you want to achieve a good, strong mix.

- Use clean aggregate that has sharp edges and is of even size. Crushed material such as gravel is ideal. Sand should consist of fine and coarse particles. Remember any dirt or vegetation will prevent the mix binding together, weakening the concrete.
- Measure the dry materials (cement and aggregate) carefully and mix them up thoroughly. Incomplete mixing will result in some parts having too much aggregate and others too little.
- Add clean water gradually, pouring it into a hollow in centre of the dry mix. Use only enough to make the mix workable; too much weakens the concrete.

Masonry retaining walls are among the most attractive, but they do not come cheap if you have to buy the stone. However, if a wall is to stay visible and not be covered with plants, the extra expense may be worth it.

MASONRY RETAINING WALL

We built our wall from ashlar masonry (stones trimmed to a regular, rectangular shape) and laid without mortar. Ashlar masonry fits together neatly, but there will be enough space between the stones to allow drainage.

Other, less regular stone shapes work equally well but as they fit together less neatly, they may not be quite as stable. Solve this problem by tipping the wall further back into the slope for stability. A sloping wall is, after all, just as attractive. The gaps between the stones can be filled with small stones wedged into the crevices or you can plant flowers or foliage plants in the gaps so that the wall has a softer, less stark appearance. Even in an ashlar wall small gaps can be left for plantings.

If you use mortar when building a masonry wall, remember to leave weep holes for drainage.

Detail of wall showing neat joins.

1 Lay out the wall with stakes and string, and then dig a shallow trench, cutting its back side at a slight angle to the slope. For drainage, lay about 25 mm of gravel in the trench. Our wall will turn a corner, but the same techniques apply to straight walls.

3 Lay succeeding courses so that each stone bridges a joint below. If you must cut a stone, use a sledge and chisel. If a stone wobbles a bit, trowel loose soil underneath.

2 Lay your longest stones on the bottom; the fewer the joints in the first course, the stronger it will be. As you lay stones, level them as best you can by tapping with the handle end of a sledge. (Remember, to avoid back injury you should bend at the knees.)

4 Dig a hole into the slope every 1.5 m and lay a long stone crosswise to the wall. Pressure from earth above these stones will tie the wall to the soil behind it.

A wooden retaining wall will quickly become part of the garden as it is weathered, especially if it is covered with cascading plants.

WOOD RETAINING WALL

For our wood retaining wall we used 200 x 200 mm timbers of treated radiata pine. Other construction grade timbers such as oregon and Australian hardwoods are also good options, but avoid old railway sleepers—these are treated with creosote, which is harmful to some plants and can make the sleepers messy to work with. Reinforcing rods hold the structure together securely.

1 Cut a bevelled trench into the slope, wet the trench and tamp well. Set the first timber in place and level it. This course will be completely buried in the ground. We planned our wall to turn a corner; the same techniques apply to a straight wall.

2 Set a second timber on top of the first and bore a hole through the two timbers. (Use a heavy duty drill with an extension bit; small drills burn out on long holes such as these.) Drive 19 mm reinforcing rod through the holes and into the ground. These rods will hold the timbers firmly together.

3 Continue to place the timbers, staggering joints from one course to the next. Drill holes and use reinforcing rod to pin each timber to the one below on each side of every joint. When needed, cut timbers with a sharp chain saw, wearing goggles to protect your eyes from flying chips.

4 Backfill as necessary. For drainage, drill weep holes every 1.2 m along the wall's length. One row of holes about 300 mm above ground is fine. Instead of drilling holes, you can provide drainage by leaving 25 mm gaps between the timbers. Plant trailing flowers above and in the crevices, if you like.

DRY STONE WALLS

Dry stone walls are built without mortar or any other bonding agent. Their strength depends solely on the selection of stones and their considered placement, along with a combination of gravity and friction. When properly built, these walls are beautiful, strong and very durable.

A dry stone wall can be built to almost any height, a rough guide being that the width of the wall under the copestone should be half that of the base. If in doubt, make the wall wider rather than narrower. Use large, flat-bottomed stones for a stable structure—the stones become progressively smaller as the wall rises.

MIND YOUR BACK
Remember these simple rules when lifting large stones:
- Work with someone else.
- Use a wheelbarrow where you can.
- Roll a stone rather than lift it where you can.
- Keep the work area clear.
- Always lift by bending your knees while keeping your back as straight as possible.

Drystone walls are attractive in themselves, as well as providing strong and durable walling. They are especially suitable for country gardens, where the stones may also be locally available.

RAISING THE WALL

1 Use string stretched taut to mark out the line of both sides of the wall. On softer ground dig a trench 10–20 cm deep so that loose earth and grass is removed. On stony or compacted ground this is not necessary as long as the site is level and free of all obstructions, such as large tree roots.

2 Build logically, placing the largest stones first, with the flattest side down. Pack around and under them with smaller stones. If there is a cavity inside the wall, fill it with one large stone rather than a lot of small ones. Never use clay, soil or screenings to fill the wall as they will weaken the structure.

3 Lay the stones so that they lie with the longer side running into the wall, not along the face. This makes a much stronger wall as less hearting material is required.

4 Use the bigger stones towards the bottom of the wall. As the wall rises it gets thinner and there may not be enough width for the big stones at the top.

5 Make sure each stone is firmly in place before moving on to the next.

6 Always cover the joints formed by the stones below, or lines of weakness (running joints) will develop.

Copestones give the top of the wall a distinctive finish and extra strength.

7 Build up both sides of the wall at the same time and keep each side roughly the same height.

8 Fill the wall as the work proceeds, that is, course by course. Do not leave it until the end of the job.

THROUGHSTONES

Throughstones are stones laid through the wall from one side to the other. In some areas large enough stones are not found and so they cannot be used, but they do help make the wall stronger. Place them at 1 m intervals along the wall, about halfway up the wall. Place the flatter side down and make sure they cover a joint on both sides of the wall.

COPESTONES

Copestones are placed along the top of the wall not only to make it more attractive but also to help bind the wall together.

Place each copestone beside the last one, but it should not be supported by it or you will create a domino effect. Each stone should be self-supporting. Once the copestones are all in place, they are pinned by taking V-shaped slices of stone and driving them into the

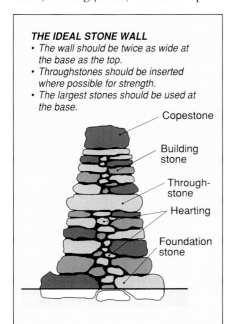

THE IDEAL STONE WALL
- The wall should be twice as wide at the base as the top.
- Throughstones should be inserted where possible for strength.
- The largest stones should be used at the base.

Copestone

Building stone

Through-stone

Hearting

Foundation stone

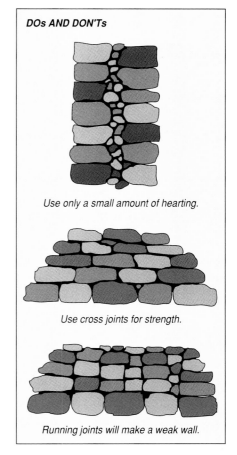

DOs AND DON'Ts

Use only a small amount of hearting.

Use cross joints for strength.

Running joints will make a weak wall.

spaces between the copestones. If this is done properly, you will be able to walk along the top of the wall without creating any movement of stones.

Information supplied by Nathan Perkins

BUILDING A TIMBER FENCE

Putting up a timber fence is a satisfying project that does not require any special skills or tools. The hardest part is digging the holes; after that the structure takes shape quickly. You will need to rent a posthole digger, but otherwise will require only a circular saw and ordinary carpentry tools.

Designs vary widely but just about all fences consist of the same basic elements: a series of posts sunk into the ground and connected by rails at the top, bottom and possibly middle as well, and palings or panels that are nailed to the railings to give the fence its character. Most fences require 100 x 100 mm posts but rails and fencing material can be almost any size. It is possible to buy prefabricated fence sections, but custom designed and built ones will usually give a better result. See page 79 for some sample fence styles.

Before beginning, check your local building and planning regulations. Many specify maximum heights, distances from property lines and the street, and even the materials you can and can't use.

PREPARING THE SITE

Once you have chosen a design and established a location, stake out and measure the site. Plot post spacing for the most efficient use of timber. Spans of about 2 m work well; never set posts for a paling or panel fence more than 2.4 m apart.

A timber paling fence is often chosen, especially for side and back fences. Although it is not the cheapest option, the natural look is attractive.

If you are building your fence on a slope, plan to step the fence down the hill, setting each section lower than the one preceding it. Build the fence to follow the contour only if the slope is very slight. In any case, be sure to set the posts vertically or the fence will look as though it is falling down the hill.

MATERIALS

In termite-prone areas always use treated timber for all posts and bottom rails. To minimise rust, buy only galvanised nails and fittings. To preserve posts, let them stand in a 20 litre pail of creosote overnight.

If you want to stain or paint your fence, apply the finish to posts, rails and fencing before you nail up the fencing. Besides saving time, you'll get better coverage.

ERECTING THE FENCE

1 Lay out the site, dig holes and set posts in concrete or anchor brackets (see page 17), starting with the end posts. Check each post for plumb by holding a level to two adjacent faces; nail braces to hold the posts upright. Check, too, that posts are aligned by tying string from end post to end post.

POST AND RAIL JOINERY TECHNIQUES

If you don't like the look of the metal rail connectors shown below in our step-by-step pictures, you can attach the rails of the fence to the posts with one of these traditional timber joints.

All of the joints will result in a satisfactory fence but each has particular qualities that you should consider, for instance the butt joint is not as strong as the others and should not be used if the fence needs to withstand any force. In that case, the mortice and tenon joint might be your best bet.

Other factors to affect your decision will be your skill in joinery and the tools you have.

1 Housing joint. Cut away part of the post so that the rail will be flush, or very nearly flush, with the post. Set the rail so that it is halfway through the housing (the next rail will fit in the other half) and nail through.

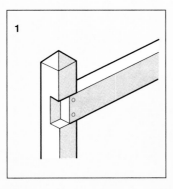

2 Block joint. Nail a short piece of 50 x 50 mm timber to the post, with its top level with the bottom of the rail, to serve as a block. Rest the rail on top of the block and skew nail through the rail and block into the post.

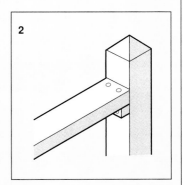

3 Butt joint. Set the end of the rail against the post at the required height, supporting the other end of the rail so that it is horizontal. Drive nails at an angle through the rail into the post. (This does not give a strong joint.)

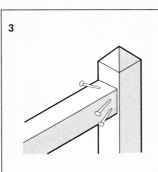

4 Mortice and tenon joint. Cut a recess or mortice in the post at the required height and trim the end of the rail to form a tenon. Place the tenon in the mortice, drill a hole from the side and hammer in a hardwood pin.

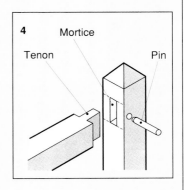

Mortice
Tenon
Pin

2 As you shovel concrete into the holes, have a helper tamp the concrete to remove bubbles. Round off the concrete so that water will drain away from the posts. After the concrete cures, cut the posts to a uniform height, if necessary. Shape the tops of the posts so that they will shed water.

3 Attach the rails to the posts. We used galvanised rail clips but see the box above for other techniques: mortice and tenon joints are, of course, the traditional methods used for fence construction in Australia. A line level and combination square ensure that each rail is level and square with the posts.

4 Measure carefully and use a square to mark locations on the rails for each fencing board. Wood scraps squeezed between the boards will maintain uniform spacing. Have a helper align the boards—in this case flush with the bottom—while you nail them to the rails. This is not an easy job for one person.

BUILDING A GATE

The simple fence and gate described on pages 76–7 and at right have here been given a more elegant appearance. The pergola with classical columns may not suit your house style, but any paling fence can be given a lift by cutting the top to shape.

1 Build a frame 10 mm narrower than the gap in the fence. Square the frame, secure corners with angle brackets and install a brace from the bottom of the hinge side to the top of the latch side.

2 Add finish boards to match the fencing. Measure carefully and install hinges, taking care that they are square with the edge. All but very lightweight gates should have three hinges.

The low height and lightweight timbers used in this picket fence have allowed a very simple gate construction. The palings are fixed to two rails, with extra blocks added below the rails at one end to take the hinges.

3 Prop the gate into position on blocks. Plumb it and have a helper mark each hinge position. Remove the gate, drill holes and hang the gate. Finally, install your latch hardware.

FENCE AND SCREEN STYLES

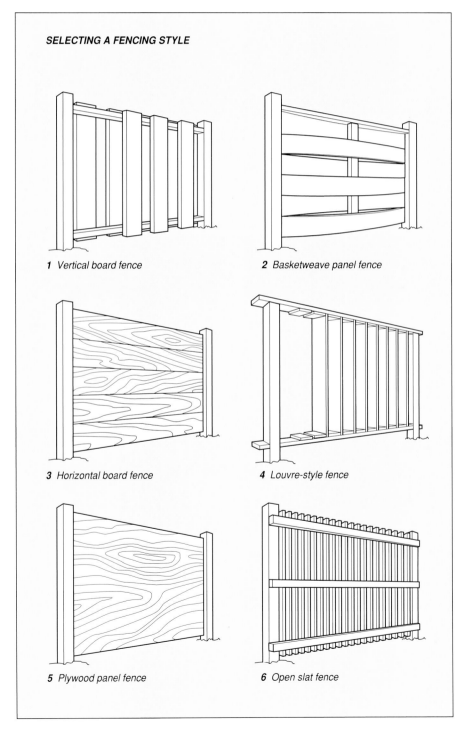

SELECTING A FENCING STYLE

1 *Vertical board fence*

2 *Basketweave panel fence*

3 *Horizontal board fence*

4 *Louvre-style fence*

5 *Plywood panel fence*

6 *Open slat fence*

Fences can give various degrees of privacy and architectural interest but they may also cut off light and breezes. Select a fence style that will satisfy your needs: louvre or lattice will let in breezes, panels and vertical board fences can give you privacy. Or combine several styles, for example a solid one below and an open one above.

1 Vertical board fences and screens are popular and easy to construct. Nail all boards to one side, as we did on pages 76–7 or alternate them as here.

2 Basketweave panels can be purchased from hardware centres and timber yards. Many also sell the vertically grooved posts into which the panels fit. Fibre cement sheeting makes the best basketweave panel.

3 Grooved posts also work well with a horizontal board design. As an alternative, you can nail boards to the posts and to 100 x 50 mm rails top and bottom.

4 Louvre-style fences and screens offer beauty and ventilation. The verticals—usually 150 x 25 or 200 x 25 mm—are angled and over-lapped slightly. The degree of the angle determines the degree of privacy you receive.

5 Fit plywood panels into grooved posts, or nail them to posts and rails. Install the panels either vertically or horizontally.

6 For an open-slat design, space 75 x 25 mm timbers their own width apart, then secure the boards at the top, bottom and middle with rails made of bigger dimension timber.

SCREENS

A garden screen is both handy and attractive. It can provide privacy from neighbours or passers-by, conceal unsightly gardening materials, give shelter from winds and enhance the appearance of the garden. Design your garden screen to do just what you want it to, remembering that an L-shaped screen is more stable than a straight one would be.

Vertical posts and horizontal slats make an effective screen, increasing the privacy of the courtyard. The screen can also support climbing plants.

SYMMETRICAL SPLENDOUR

This project is as simple as 1, 2, 3—even for the beginner. Use dressed oregon or treated pine—stained or painted to match your house style—for an effective result.

1 Dig three cubic post holes, each 300 x 300 x 300 mm. Fill each post hole with mixed cement and set a post support in place in each. Use a 30 mm thick piece of timber to span across the top of the footing pad, under the plate of the post support, to hold the support 30 mm out of the cement (see diagram opposite).

2 Drill holes, the same size as the rod of the support, in the bottom of the posts. This will ensure the posts fit tightly. Hammer the posts down over the supports from the top, making sure they are square with each other.

3 Use 91 x 19 mm horizontals and position them up the posts with 70 mm gaps. Fasten the horizontals with two 70 mm countersunk screws (brass are best as they won't stain the timber) at each end. Finish with external stain, if desired.

MATERIALS LIST

Three 100 x 100 mm timber posts 2.5 m long, sixteen 91 x 19 mm horizontals 2.0 m* long and sixteen 1.0 m* long, scraps of 30 mm thick timber, at least 500 mm long; two 25 kg bags of sand and cement mix; three post supports with dowel but no side plates; 128 countersunk 70 mm screws.

*Adjust the length to fit your site.

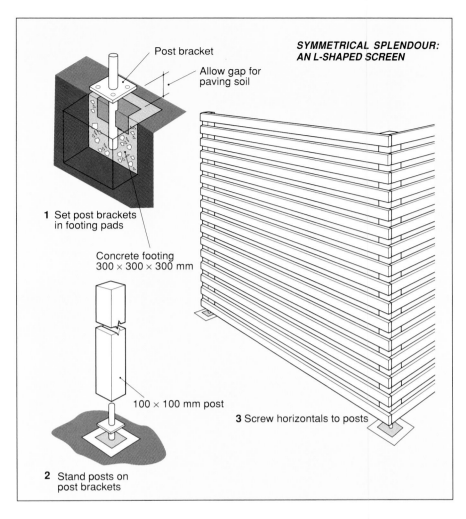

SYMMETRICAL SPLENDOUR: AN L-SHAPED SCREEN

Post bracket

Allow gap for paving soil

1 Set post brackets in footing pads

Concrete footing 300 × 300 × 300 mm

100 × 100 mm post

3 Screw horizontals to posts

2 Stand posts on post brackets

GARDEN TIDY
Prefabricated louvre panels fixed to a timber frame form the basis of this tidy. Decide on the size of tidy you need and then purchase the louvre panels. It is easier to adapt the framework to the panels than the panels to the framework.

Top trim 75 × 12 mm

Shelf support

50 × 50 mm

This neat garden tidy has a built-in shelf for pot plants so that garbage bins are hidden from above as well as from the side.

TIDY UP THE GARDEN

A simple and effective way to improve the appearance of your house is to build a tidy such as the one shown below. The low screen and shelf for pot plants will shield your garbage bins from all eyes, and the prefabricated louvre doors allow air to circulate around the bins. We built an L-shaped screen against the house, but it is easy to add another end if a free-standing structure will suit your situation better. If you have a large, wheeled bin, enlarge the tidy so that it is 1350 mm high and 820 mm deep.

1 Starting from the prefabricated louvre panels, calculate the dimensions of the screen. We used 1000 x 520 mm panels and so the frame is 520 mm deep, 1040 mm long and 1000 mm high.

2 Erect the sides, using uprights between each louvred panel, and inserting between the end uprights a shelf support 250 mm down from the top. Fix a corresponding support to the house wall.

3 Nail the shelf slats to the supports, spacing them so as to allow for drainage.

4 Add external corner battens as shown in the diagram. Add a top trim, mitred at the corner and nailed to the tops of the uprights as well as to the louvred screens.

5 Finish by painting or staining the screen so that it fits the style of the house and is well protected from any bad weather.

MATERIALS LIST

Component	Size (mm)	Length (mm)	No.
Louvre door	1000		3
	x 520		
Frame uprights	50 x 50	1000	4
Shelf support	50 x 50	520	2
Shelf slats	75 x 12	1040	
Top trim	75 x 12	1040	1
	75 x 12	520	1
Corner battens	30 x 30	1000	1

LATTICE SCREENS

Designs for screens can be varied but for a really striking effect, consider lacy latticework screens, which provide privacy without blocking summer breezes. Lattice screens also offer sound support for climbing plants, which increases privacy even more. Lattice is not expensive and demands no special expertise to build—you can install it with only simple hand tools and an electric drill/driver.

The term 'lattice' refers to any decorative pattern made with narrow, thin strips of wood (see page 84 for different lattice styles). Lattice designed primarily for privacy has 38 mm openings; for garden-spaced lattice the openings are 76 mm wide. If you are using lattice for a trellis or arbour overhead it will need to be stronger than usual: use 50 x 25 mm strips instead of laths.

Be innovative in your use of lattice. For example, as well as fences and freestanding screens, try using attached panels to support plants and shade a western-facing wall.

These lattice panels are attached to the eaves, shading the wall from the afternoon sun and supporting climbing plants.

PREFABRICATED PANELS

Most timberyards and hardware stores sell prefabricated lattice panels for a cost that is often less than that for the laths alone. These panels are easy to install because the cutting and nailing are already done.

Inspect the panels carefully before you buy. Cheaper varieties are often made with lath that is much thinner than that sold in individual pieces, and the staples holding cheap lattice together may be thin and dislodge easily. Although most are made from treated pine and so are resistant to termites, they will rot eventually.

HOMEMADE LATTICE PANELS

1 Build the frame as described below and, if desired, paint or stain the frame and the strips of lath. If you prefer to leave the wood natural, coat it with a wood preservative.
2 Lay the lath against the frame diagonally, placing the strips so that each strip touches the next to form a solid screen. Nail every second strip (or every third for garden-spaced lattice) and then remove the pieces not nailed. To avoid splitting the extra-thin strips, blunt the tips of nails by pounding on them with a hammer before using them.
3 Repeat this process for the second course of lattice, starting at the opposite corner.
4 Trim the ends with a cross-cut or circular saw.

BUILDING A SCREEN

1 After you have set the posts, measure the distance between them and build a frame from 100 x 50 mm timber. Square each corner, using temporary wood braces to hold the corners square. Then nail the frame together at each corner.

2 Remove the braces one by one, check each corner again with a square, and secure the joint with a metal strip or angle. As with all outdoor work, use only galvanised screws and hardware to avoid rust and staining of the wood.

3 Now attach the first stop of 25 x 25 mm timber to the inner side of the frame. Align it with one edge. Predrill holes at intervals of 300 mm or so, and drive screws through the 25 x 25 mm timber and into the frame itself.

4 Take a prefabricated panel or make your own lattice as described above. Make sure it fits precisely into the frame, trimming the edges as necessary to fit. If you have not yet done so, paint or stain the lattice and frame.

5 After the paint dries, lay the panel atop the frame's first stop, then install a second stop on top of the panel. If desired, attach the lattice to the first stop with a staple gun before adding the second stop. This makes for easier handling.

6 Fasten the frame to the posts with coach screws spaced about 300 mm apart. Predrill holes and, for a neater appearance, countersink them as well. Fit each coach screw with a washer before driving it. Touch up paint.

LATTICE STYLES

Latticework lends itself to a variety of decorative effects. Choose a style that suits your home and the purpose to which you will put it—privacy screen, support for climbing plants, or windbreak. And then varnish or paint it, as desired.

1 Provide a contrast of round and square openings by boring holes at the points where strips intersect.
2 Vertical and horizontal strips make a strong grid pattern, which can be emphasised by using laths with a rough texture and variations in thickness. Such rough lattice can be constructed from 'fall-down' laths, the inexpensive wood left over when timber is milled.

3 Notched lattice strips create an interesting and decorative design. You can purchase panels of notched lattice, buy notched strips or notch the strips yourself.
4 Garden-spaced lattice is more open than normal lattice. It doesn't provide a lot of privacy until vines begin to flourish but if you want to let through breezes or just support plants it is ideal.

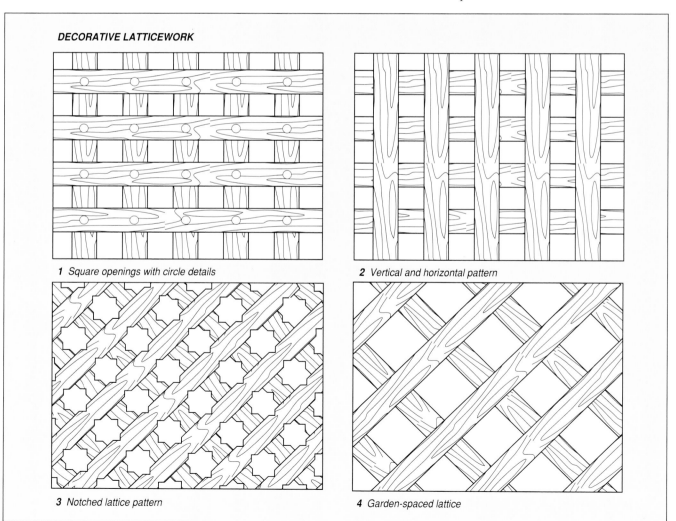

DECORATIVE LATTICEWORK

1 Square openings with circle details

2 Vertical and horizontal pattern

3 Notched lattice pattern

4 Garden-spaced lattice

Lattice can transform a balcony, giving it an elegant and individual look. Use it for its own decorative qualities, train vines up it or hang plants from it, as here. The lattice is a perfect complement to this older style balcony, but even a modern unit balcony can be transformed with lattice against a blank end wall.

PATHS, PAVING AND

In many ways, grass is the ideal surface for a garden. Quiet and soft underfoot, it absorbs glare and heat, and there is no better surface for children to play on. But it does get soggy after rain, it doesn't like growing in heavy shade, and it won't take an infinite amount of traffic. So even the greenest of country gardens will need some paving, to make patios and terraces to sit out on, paths to lead from one part of the garden to the other, and steps that are safe and easy-to-use.

Which material you choose for your paved areas will depend on the style of the garden—gravel, for instance, is informal and rustic, squared stone very formal, plain concrete reminiscent of roads and service stations, concrete with an exposed aggregate finish rather less austere. It depends on your budget too—paving is a big item in the cost of making a garden—but happily you can save a lot by doing it yourself. Paving isn't difficult, just heavy work, calling for strong backs and refreshment after the job is done.

While you're shifting earth, why not think about a pond? It isn't difficult or expensive to make one. The sight and sound of water is wonderfully refreshing, and water plants and fish add a new dimension to gardening. Your water garden could be the focal point of the whole garden design.

A paved area is a lovely place to sit and enjoy your garden. Here paving swirls between the garden beds in innovative designs.

PONDS

The gentle splash of water provides a refreshing atmosphere in any garden. Clever use of stones and water plants will give a natural-looking effect.

Paving need not be formal—even a small, irregular area of stones set in pebbles will enrich your outdoor living style.

BASICS OF PAVING

Paths and paving are more than just functional—they are as important to the look of your garden as floor coverings are to the house. The range of possible paving materials is vast, and so before choosing one think carefully about how your garden is used and the style you want it to have. Consider ease of laying, but don't let that be the overriding factor in your choice.

It's a good idea to standardise materials and tie them into existing structures or features. For instance, brick pavers will give an integrated, wrap-around feel to a brick house. For bush gardens, aim for natural-looking materials, such as informal stone paving. You can use gravel, bark chips or natural leaf litter for less trodden paths.

As a rule, stone is the most expensive paving material because of the cost of skilled laying. Concrete and unit pavers (brick, concrete cobblestones) occupy the mid-range while loose surface materials such as gravel or pine bark are the cheapest.

The right preparation is vital. Careful groundwork will pay dividends in durability and appearance. A poorly prepared base can soon cause cracking or billowing of the surface. In time, this means costly repairs, plus an area that is unsafe and unattractive.

Paving stones and pebbles are set in concrete to make this durable path. Nonetheless, the impression is of a natural path made by constant wear.

PLANNING PATHS

Paths should always be functional and convenient. As a rule, service paths leading to a shed, barbecue or clothesline should follow the most direct route. Walk along the line you would naturally take and plan your path to follow that route or people will not use it. It will usually be a straight line but may be deflected by dips and rises in the ground. You can, of course, be more creative when laying out a path for strolling.

Don't skimp on width: main paths should be at least 1.5 m wide and preferably 1.8 m, so that two people can pass each other on the path in comfort.

Flagstones, stepping stones and crazy paving. This style of paving is good-looking, durable and suited to most styles of garden. However, creating a pleasing arrangement is trickier than you might think and the irregular thickness of the pavers can make laying fiddly. This style of paving can also be fairly expensive over large areas.

Bricks. Bricks come in a wide range of colours and can be laid in many patterns. Relatively inexpensive, they will suit any garden, are easy to lay and will take the weight of cars. Beware of old, soft bricks as they can stain easily or crumble, and ensure the base is well prepared. Cutting bricks is tedious, so choose the laying pattern carefully.

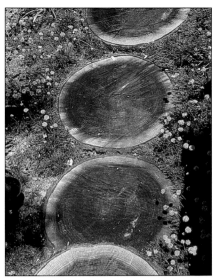

Tree rounds. Inexpensive and easy to lay, tree rounds are best suited for paths that don't get a lot of use in wild or bush gardens. They are not very durable and do not look particularly attractive if laid over large areas. Their informal appearance does, however, make them especially suitable for use in areas that you don't want to look formal.

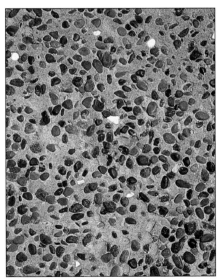

Concrete. This is relatively inexpensive, very easy to lay in any shape, durable and quite attractive with exposed aggregate or pressed pattern finish. However, like bricks, concrete must be laid on a sound surface or it will crack. If the concrete is poorly laid, very hot weather will also crack it. Combine it with other surfaces for variety.

Gravel. Loose gravel is very easy to lay and attractive in an informal setting. It is, however, uncomfortable for bare feet and is awkward to walk on if laid too deeply (3 cm is sufficient). It is not suitable for slopes, as it washes away during heavy rain, nor is it a good choice near lawns as the stones will scatter into the grass.

Concrete pavers. These come in a wide choice of colours and shapes, are relatively inexpensive and durable and are able to withstand vehicular traffic. However, they do stain easily (and so think about the possibility of motor oil or barbecue fat dripping on them) and they must be laid over a well-prepared base or good, flat surface.

BRICK PATHS AND PAVING

HOW TO LAY BRICKS AND PAVERS

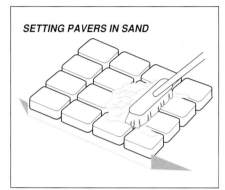

SETTING PAVERS IN SAND

1 Excavate the route of the path (or the area of the pavement) to the depth of the paving units plus about 25 mm more.

2 Build edgings along the path or around the area. Use timber strips, concrete strips or concreted pavers.

3 Compact the soil and lay a 25–50 mm thick bed of sand, tamping it down and levelling it with a length of straight timber. Coarse bush sand is less likely to wash out.

4 Lay the paving units tightly in your selected pattern. Consolidate the pavers with a rubber mallet or bricklayer's hammer and the length of straight-edged timber to maintain level. Alternatively, pavers can be laid on a bed of sand and cement or on a concrete slab. Check the manufacturer's instructions.

BRICK PATTERNS

Bricks can be laid in many patterns, from simple to complex. As standard bricks are 230 x 110 x 75 mm, they are difficult to lay in regular patterns—specially made paving bricks are easier to use.

This brick patio creates a beautiful outdoor room that is ideal for summer living. The bricks are laid in herringbone pattern, with a row of stretchers at one end, and they are kept in place with a timber framework.

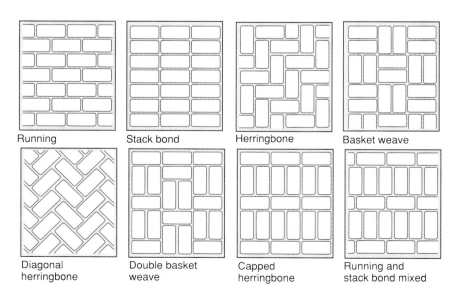

Running

Stack bond

Herringbone

Basket weave

Diagonal herringbone

Double basket weave

Capped herringbone

Running and stack bond mixed

A tempting path is made from bricks and sandstone pavers laid in sand and kept in place with timber framework. The alternating materials break up the line of the path and give an impression that the path is disappearing into the distance.

The patio surrounding this pool is laid in basket weave pattern and is bordered by cemented paving stones. The soft, mottled colours provide a mellow and traditional look for the area.

The traditional style of the house is complemented by the brick patio laid in simple running pattern. It provides a pleasant, level area for entertaining, family meals or just sitting.

PAVING STONES

MAKING A PATH

Stepping stones can be used to make a very attractive and practical path—and it isn't too difficult to do! Just plan the route of the path as explained on page 88 and lay out the stones on the surface to make sure you have enough.

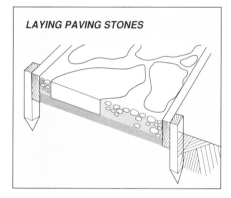

LAYING PAVING STONES

1 Excavate the route of the path to the depth of the stones plus 25 mm.
2 Build forms of 100 x 25 mm timber inside the edges of the excavated path, and retain them in place with timber stakes nailed to the outside (see diagram above). Alternatively, use brick, stone, treated logs or sleepers to edge the area.
3 Compact the base of the path and cover it with roadbase to a depth of 25 mm. Tamp the roadbase until the surface is hard.
4 Set stones in 25 mm of sand (or weak mortar if you are using thin stone—mix one part each of cement and lime to twelve parts sand). Tap into place with a rubber mallet. Fill in the surrounding space with pea gravel, pine bark or mortar until it is level with the surface of the paving stones.

Use concrete squares as pavers to create a quick and easy path. Here they are laid in a diamond pattern for added effect. Use the steps given above to lay them, and use string lines to get the alignment correct.

DRIVE-IN STEPPING STONES

Driveways need not always be solid strips of concrete. A wide pathway of flagstones set in lawn is a stylish solution. Set the stones on individual concrete islands for stability and to prevent cracking. Car traffic trims the grass edges, but you will need to aerate the grass regularly with a garden fork.

1 Place stones in the desired positions and mark the outlines with a knife or spade.

2 Remove the stones and cut holes in the ground as deep as the stones plus 25 mm. Mix the cement, lime and sand in a ratio of 1:1:12 in a runny consistency.

3 Bed the stones carefully on the mortar, using a mallet and spirit level to keep them level.

4 Once the mortar has dried, allow grass to regrow around the stones or cut turf to fit.

This useful paved area has been created with large slabs of flattish stone set in a mix of pebbles. Prepare the area as described for paths (see opposite) and place the stones on the sand so that they are almost touching. Pack pebbles in the areas between so that you create a level surface.

Paving stones set in grass form an unusual and attractive driveway.

Hint

When mixing cement for topping or mortar, add lime (one part to one part cement and six parts sand) to make the mix more plastic. Commercial preparations such as Bycol can be used instead of lime or, if you have neither handy, you can use a squirt of liquid detergent in the water.

A more formal area has been created by setting the paving stones in concrete. Prepare the area as described for paths but use a 25 mm thick layer of concrete instead of sand. Set the stones in place and fill the interstices with more concrete.

CONCRETE PATHS

Concrete can be used alone or in combination with any number of materials to create some very attractive surfaces.

A CONCRETE PATH

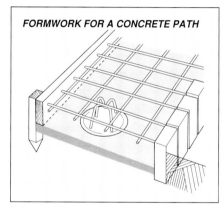

FORMWORK FOR A CONCRETE PATH

1 Excavate the route of the path to about 150 mm depth.
2 Build forms of 100 x 25 mm timber held in place by 50 x 25 mm stakes. Use several hardboard strips for curves or retain concrete with permanent edging of brick, stone or treated timber.
3 Compact the soil, and then lay a 25–50 mm bed of sand and level it with a straight-edge.
4 Lay Weldmesh F62 on bar chairs at half the depth of the path.
5 Wet removable forms and shovel in mixed concrete. Level it with straight-edged timber. Smooth the surface with a wooden trowel. Allow excess water to rise to the surface and evaporate, and then use a steel trowel for a smooth finish. If exposed aggregate finish is desired, add pebbles at this stage.

6 Run control joint grooves at regular intervals along the path so as to prevent it cracking.
7 If you have added aggregate, use a wide, stiff broom or wire brush and a fine spray from the hose to clean off the pebbles when the concrete is partially dry. If you have to walk over the concrete, use a plank.
8 Cover the path with moist hessian and leave it in place for seven days. (This helps prevent cracking.) Remove temporary forms once the concrete has dried for at least twenty-four hours.

A CONSOLIDATED PATH

A path of consolidated tennis court loam is ideal in a natural garden, especially in drier areas. Border it with stone or logs and let ground-covers encroach on the edges.
1 Excavate the route of the path to a depth of 50–75 mm. Apply earth or roadbase and ram it down to a depth of 25 mm.
2 Build forms of 100 x 25 mm timber inside the edges of the excavated path and retain them in place with stakes nailed to the outside.

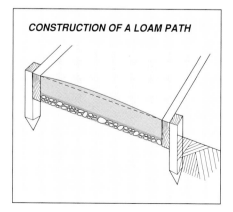

CONSTRUCTION OF A LOAM PATH

Alternatively, use brick, stone, treated logs or sleepers to form more permanent edgings.
3 Thoroughly mix dry tennis court loam with cement in the ratio of 10 parts loam to 1 part cement.
4 Keeping some of the mixture in reserve, lay the rest of it dry between the edgings. Smooth the surface, leaving a slight camber for drainage. Use a straight-edged timber to ensure the sides of the path are on an even plane.
5 Consolidate the surface with roller or rammer. Fill any depressions with the reserved mix.
6 Using a fine mist spray, thoroughly saturate the area and let the water soak in.
7 Repeat the rolling or ramming process until the path is compressed. Do not walk on the area for several days.

Consolidated loam makes a path that is really natural looking.

NATURAL PATHS

Loose materials such as gravel can be cheap as well as attractive.

Loose materials such as pea gravel and bark chips can make attractive, natural-looking paths for less formal gardens or, in the case of gravel, even formal situations.

1 Mark out the path and remove soil to a depth of 50–75 mm.

2 Edge the path with formwork of 100 x 25 mm timber bedded to the level required. Hold it in place with strong timber stakes nailed to the outside. Alternatively, use brick, stone, treated logs or other permanent edging.

3 Saturate the path and lay 25 mm of roadbase along the full length (in light, sandy soils lay 50–70 mm). Moisten and consolidate the area with a roller or rammer. The base must be firm.

4 When the base material ceases to sink into the soil, fill the path with your loose material and grade.

Alternatively, if you have a level surface, you can prepare the path area as described in steps 1 and 2, and then cover the base of the path with shadecloth tucked under the edgings. Peg any joins with bent wire to prevent the shadecloth lifting, and cover it with 30 mm of gravel or chips.

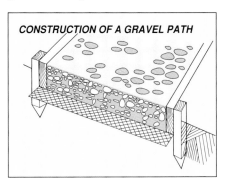

CONSTRUCTION OF A GRAVEL PATH

Loose materials have been used to advantage in this courtyard to create a natural and yet mannered appearance. Large stones drift away from the main paved area into the gravel so that the line between the materials is soft and not abrupt.

INSTALLING PATH EDGINGS

For only a modest investment of time and money, edgings can be used to dress up a plain path, provide crisp lines between paving and landscaping materials or hold paving blocks or bricks in place. In most cases you simply decide on the material you'd like to use, excavate shallow trenches on either side of the walk, and stake or set the edging in place. (One exception is integral concrete edging (see opposite) which is installed at the same time as the path.)

Edging materials can vary just as much as the pavings they border. Choose from concrete, brick, stone, tile, wood or vinyl. Edging styles, however, fall into just two broad categories: a raised edging that puts a lip at each side of a walk or path, or a mowing strip that is installed flush with the path so that you can run one wheel of a lawnmower along it.

MOWING STRIPS

Mowing strips should be 150–300 mm wide. Concrete, brick, tile and other smooth-surface masonry materials are best for mowing strips. You can use timbers, but be warned that they are easily nicked by the mower blade and will rot away over time.

RAISED EDGINGS

A raised edging keeps aggressive groundcover from growing over a path, channels water run-off and makes a clean break between different surfaces. If you are planning a path of gravel, mulch or other loose-fill material, a raised edging is the only way to go.

Keep a raised edging low, 10 mm or so, or make it 75 mm or more high. Anything in between can easily be tripped over. In the sections below and opposite we give instructions for installing several types of raised edgings.

WOOD EDGING

1 Dig a trench alongside the path. Make it about 90 mm deep, deep enough to accommodate 10 mm of gravel and all but 10 mm of a 75 x 38 mm timber. The gravel bed should be about 250 mm wide for adequate drainage. This will prevent premature rotting of the timber.

2 Lay the gravel bed, and then stake 75 x 38 mm boards in place. Mitre-cut end-to-end joints to make them less conspicuous. Drive in nails for the stakes so that their tops will be about 25 mm below the top edges of the boards. Projecting stakes can be dangerous.

3 Backfill with enough topsoil to cover the stakes. Compact the soil, and then cover it with sod, if you want your lawn to continue right up the path, or mulch. Or you may prefer to create a garden beside the path, planting in it any good edging plant to soften the edges.

INTEGRAL CONCRETE EDGING

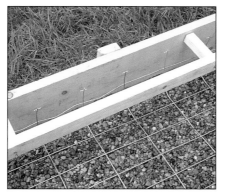

1 Construct plywood forms at the edge of your planned path. For a 90 mm thick path, leave a 90 mm gap between the gravel bed and inside board. Temporarily nail short pieces of wood between the inside and outside boards. Stake forms every 900 mm or so.

2 Lay reinforcing mesh, bending it so that its tips stick up into the curb forms. These tie the path and edging into an integral unit that will ride out settling. When you pour the concrete, pull the mesh into the middle of the slab and curb with a claw hammer or rake.

3 Pour concrete into the edging forms first, then into the path area, pulling out wood spacers as you pour. Strike off and trowel the surface but do not make it too smooth or it may become slippery. Let the concrete cure for a week, and then remove stakes and forms.

BRICK EDGING

Bricks are possibly the most popular path edging, whether set on edge, on end or at an angle to create a sawtooth effect. They are excellent borders for concrete, loose materials or, of course, brick paving. Choose colours that match or contrast with the path surface.

The brick edging should be set in sand or mortared to a concrete base. See the section on brick paving (pages 90–1). Make sure the edging is firmly set in place or bricks will soon work loose.

Neat and tidy brick edgings can provide the perfect edging for most types of paths. They can be set upright or on edge as well as diagonally.

VINYL EDGING

Because it is flexible and easily curved, vinyl edging is particularly suitable for curving and irregular paths. Although the range of colours is limited, it can be used with almost any surfacing material and softened with plantings.

This is the easiest edging to install. Simply slice cuts next to the paving with a spade and then press or stake the vinyl in place. Be careful to keep the mower away from the vinyl.

Vinyl may not be the most attractive edging material but it is practical and easy to install. Use it for edgings that will be covered with plants.

BUILDING STEPS

Properly constructed garden steps not only connect different levels in the garden, they also serve as a retaining wall. They must be carefully planned and securely anchored into the slope.

Select materials to match or contrast with the walkways at top and bottom. Steps can be built from brick, concrete, timber or any combination of these materials. Or for a natural look you can terrace the slope with timber risers and surface the treads with gravel, wood chips or other loose fill.

LAYING OUT

Whatever materials you choose, you must first decide how many steps you will need, how deep each horizontal tread will be, and how high to make each vertical riser. Here's a useful hint: the tread dimension plus the riser dimension should equal about 430 mm. (*Building Code of Australia 91* specifies that the tread

Slabs of flat stone pave these wide steps to create a formal look for the garden. Their appearance has been softened by planting tiny succulents in the crevices.

plus twice the riser must fall between 585 and 700 mm.) Try to make your riser dimension no more than 180 mm and no less than 100 mm. No matter how you juggle the figures, make sure all treads and risers will be exactly the same depth and height: changes break a person's stride and cause stumbles. Also, when planning a concrete foundation be sure to take into account the depth of tread-finishing materials and mortar.

Use stakes and a level string or board to determine the total rise your steps will ascend and the total run they will traverse (see section on page 35). To determine how many steps you will need, divide these measurements by various combinations of tread and riser sizes until you have equal-size steps. A handrail is necessary if the flight exceeds five risers.

PAVED STEPS

The method described below can be used for any paving materials— pavers, bricks, stone slabs or small concrete slabs.

BRICK STEPS

1 Mark the dimensions of each step with string, and then carefully cut into the slope, digging deeper under the bottom tread for an integral footing. Mark and dig the space for each tread 50 mm or so longer than the tread will be so that the forms can overlap as shown in step 2.

2 Construct forms so that the front edge of each tread will be double thickness. Pour gravel into the forms, and then add reinforcing mesh. Suspend horizontal reinforcing rod at the points where treads and risers will meet; tie the bottom tread to its footing with vertical reinforcing rod.

3 Shovel and pour wet concrete into the forms. Poke the mix periodically with a piece of reinforcing rod to remove air pockets. Lift the mesh midway into the concrete's thickness. Strike off and trowel. Let the concrete cure for about a week, and then remove the forms. The steps are now ready for the pavers.

4 Spread a 10 mm thick bed of mortar over the riser and tread of one step. Screed the bed, and then press the pavers into place, first on the riser and then on the tread below. A string line keeps them level.

5 If a brick is too high, tap it into level with the handle of a hammer or trowel. If it's too low, lift it out and trowel on more mortar to the bottom of the brick. Use 10 mm spacers to maintain even gaps between bricks.

6 Pack grout between the bricks; tool with a joint rake or piece of pipe. When the grouting is almost dry, clean the bricks with water and a sponge. To prevent bricks being loosened, do not walk on the steps for at least a week.

COMBINATION STEPS

These steps use three different building materials to make shapes and forms that are decorative in themselves. The framework consists of 150 x 75 mm hardwood, with prefabricated pavers (we used 400 x 200 x 200 mm ones available from landscape suppliers) and we used blue metal crushed to about 10 mm for the infill of the steps.

1 Mark out the dimensions of each step with string and carefully cut out the steps.

2 Drill and nail the framework for each step together so that the timber on the edge of the tread runs the full length of the tread. The frames should be about twice as wide as the desired tread width.

3 Place the frames on the cut-out steps and skew nail them to each other as shown in the diagram.

4 Fill frames with gravel and position the pavers within the gravel.

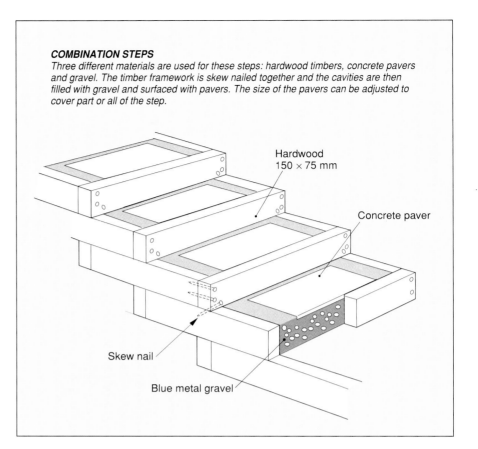

COMBINATION STEPS
Three different materials are used for these steps: hardwood timbers, concrete pavers and gravel. The timber framework is skew nailed together and the cavities are then filled with gravel and surfaced with pavers. The size of the pavers can be adjusted to cover part or all of the step.

Hardwood
150 × 75 mm

Concrete paver

Skew nail

Blue metal gravel

The timber frames of these combination steps are ideal for use on an uneven slope as the timbers can be lengthened where necessary to extend into the slope. As the materials weather, the steps will blend into the garden.

The gradual slope of this garden has been accentuated by the winding brick path. The low steps consist of frameworks of timber with brick infill to match the path. The timber frameworks are fixed securely to the path edging, which is also of large timbers, so there is no possibility of movement.

TIMBER STEPS

Timber steps can take many forms, from a staircase such as that described on pages 36–8 to the simple steps at right. Use only construction grade timbers (see box on page 35) and ones that are suitable for outdoor use, for example treated radiata pine or hardwoods. Check the steps regularly for rot as rotten steps can cause accidents.

Timber is, however, relatively simple to work with and timber steps can be constructed quickly. They also blend easily into a natural or informal setting.

1 Cut carefully into the slope, making room for the desired tread and riser dimensions. Each of our steps consisted of two 200 x 200 mm timbers with an overlap of 100 mm (that is, a tread width of 300 mm). Lay the timbers, pound them into place with a sledge and check for level.

2 Using an electrician's extension bit, bore holes at the front edge of each timber into the one below it, and then pound in reinforcing rod to tie them together. Also bore horizontal holes to secure each timber to the one behind it. These rods will hold the steps firmly together and prevent any movement.

BUILDING A RAMP

A ramp makes a gentle transition from one level to another, smoothing the path for everything from wheelbarrows to—most especially—wheelchairs. If you have a family member or friend who relies on a wheelchair, you will need a ramp to approach at least one of your house's entrances and possibly to reach outdoor areas.

You can use a variety of materials for a ramp, including concrete, wood or even earth topped with fine gravel. Do, however, make sure the surface is non-skid. Textured rubber toppings, such as skid-resistant polymer and plastic coatings, and textured concrete work well.

Where the slope is not great, a ramp is a practical alternative to steps, allowing easier access for people with limited mobility.

BUILDING A CONCRETE RAMP

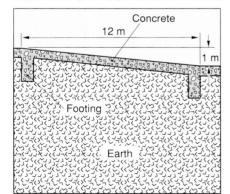

1 Use string to lay out your ramp, planning it according to the directions given opposite. A concrete ramp must tie into the slope with footings on either side of each landing. In colder areas dig the footings to the frost line. Make the ramp at least 100 mm thick.

2 We extended our ramp down from an existing slab, which we fitted with a piece of expansion strip. Cut and fill earth as necessary. Construct forms with 100 x 50 mm timber. Double check that the forms do not slope more than desired. Add gravel and reinforcing mesh.

3 Tie in footings with reinforcing rod. Pour concrete. Use a slightly stiffer mix than you would for a level slab so that the concrete will hold the incline. Strike off. Float with a darby float. Define edges with an edging trowel, and then tool control joints every 1 m or so.

RAMP BASICS

Safety and ease of use are the prime considerations for any ramp. Appearance, though, also plays a part in the design.

Slope a wheelchair ramp at no more than 1:12. This can result in very long ramps (a total rise of 1 m, for example, requires a length of at least 12 m) but a gentle grade is essential for the people who will need it most. Even if your ramp won't be used by anyone in a wheelchair, slope it no more than 1:8.

For wheelchair use, include handrails on both sides of the ramp and make the ramp wide enough so that the distance between the handrails is at least 900 mm. Landings should be placed at top and bottom and any incline longer than about 7 m needs an extra landing where a wheelchair user can rest and manoeuvre the chair. Whether your plan calls for an L-shaped, switchback or broken straight-run ramp, all landings must be as long as the path is wide but not less than 900 mm long. Where doors open outward, the landing must be at least 1.5 x 2.0 m to allow the wheelchair user to move back.

4 To make your ramp skidproof, pull a damp broom across the surface of the just-trowelled concrete. For a fine texture, use a soft-bristled broom; for a coarser one, use a stiffer bristle. Let the concrete cure for at least a week before removing the forms.

INSTALLING HANDRAILS

If you are building a ramp that will be used by people in wheelchairs, fit handrails to both sides so that they can pull themselves up. The handrails should be about 865 mm high and have a grip width of about 38 mm. On stairways install a handrail on at least one side. It should be at least 865 mm high.

To attach wooden railings to a wooden ramp, follow the instructions for fitting railings to a raised deck (page 38) and be sure to fix the balusters securely to the ramp's structure, not its surface. Similarly for wooden steps, attach the railing to the structure, not the treads.

To fix a metal railing to a concrete ramp, first drill holes into the ramp's surface (or into a concrete curb along its edge, as shown here). Install the brackets with lead masonry anchors and screws. Slip the vertical balusters into the brackets, and tighten set screws. Install the rails top and bottom and assemble the intermediate balusters. For concrete steps, attach the rail brackets to the treads.

Metal handrails are a practical option, especially for a concrete ramp or steps. They can be fixed to the curb or surface of a ramp but must be fixed to the treads of steps.

RAISED AND SUNKEN GARDENS

You can make your garden more interesting by providing occasional changes in level. By raising a garden or lowering a paved space you can create small enclosures that are ideal as sheltered, outdoor living spaces, especially when a retaining wall can double as bench seating. On the other hand, you may like to create a sunken haven for shade-loving plants or an elevated patch of lawn to act as a suntrap.

Start by taking note of the shape of the garden, the position of the house and large trees, and especially the existing contours. Then decide which areas could be lowered or effectively raised, and whether the shape should be circular, square or irregular. The basis of any raised or sunken garden is a retaining wall—here we show you a few techniques you can adapt to your own garden.

VERTICAL TIMBER WALLS
Narrow timber logs set into the ground can be used to make a retaining wall for curved shapes as well as straight ones. As long as they are properly set into the soil, vertical logs, either circular or square, will withstand any amount of stress from the soil and the moisture it contains, especially if you combine them with wooden pavers to keep the logs in place.

For a 300–350 mm high wall you should allow 150 mm of log below ground level. You can make the paving in a similar manner from shorter logs. To be solid and unmoving, they should be at least 100 mm long and tightly packed. Lay the paving first and then use the deeper wall logs to wedge the pavers in place. Build up the soil behind the retainers. To be large enough for several people to lounge in, a circular pit should have a diameter of at least 3 m.

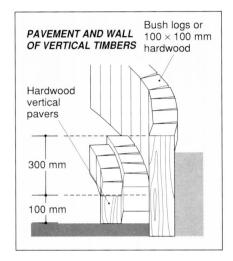

PAVEMENT AND WALL OF VERTICAL TIMBERS

Bush logs or 100 × 100 mm hardwood

Hardwood vertical pavers

300 mm

100 mm

Timber verticals and paving create an unusual sitting area, sunk into the surrounding slope. Drainage of such an area needs to be carefully planned.

HARDWOOD RETAINERS

Large hardwood slabs can be used to construct a self-contained structure that supports itself and its contents in all directions. Use 100 mm deep slabs (either recycled or new) and join them at the corners with half-lap joints (see the diagram below). As you proceed, drill and insert spikes from each layer through to the one below. Add a 150 mm wide capping timber to the top to serve as a ledge seat.

By constructing retaining walls in a large U-shape (right) you can have a large raised bed enclosing a small sunken area. This is an ideal way to make a paved spot surrounded by planting. To have a 2.5 m square paved area surrounded by 2.5 m wide raised beds, you will need to have an area of 7.5 x 5 m. If you don't have that much space to devote to the project, make the beds narrower, but don't reduce the paved space too much or it will be too small to use comfortably.

Raised beds surrounded by hardwood slabs are used to vary the ground level and provide interest, as well as a sheltered sitting spot, in this garden.

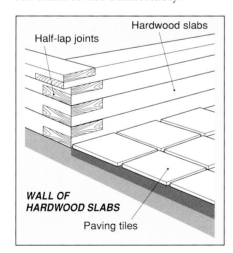

Hardwood slabs

Half-lap joints

WALL OF HARDWOOD SLABS

Paving tiles

STONE WALLING

The walls of your raised or sunken garden can also be constructed of stone. Choose flattish stones and embed the lowest course in the ground, in a shallow foundation trench. Use the larger stones in the lower courses. If your wall is to be more than three or four courses high, see the section on retaining walls on pages 70–3.

In a formal garden neatly trimmed stones can be used for a pleasing wall and steps. Here they lead down to a shallow sunken area.

GARDEN PONDS

There's nothing more soothing than a water feature. The right pond in the right place can be exceptionally appealing in any garden and the wide range of pool types and sizes allows you to select one to suit your particular situation.

FINDING A SITE

If you plan to keep fish or grow water lilies, site your pond where it gets at least five hours of full sun a day. Otherwise, its position should be influenced by the slope and style of your garden. Water will naturally flow to and collect in the lowest part of the garden and a pond will look most natural there. If that site is inconvenient, however, place the pond where it will be seen to best advantage. If you want to incorporate a fountain or cascade, or if you want to filter the water, a nearby power point will be needed.

CHOOSING SIZE AND SHAPE

When it comes to ponds, the bigger and deeper the better. Small pools evaporate quickly and the temperature of the water fluctuates too widely for the comfort of fish and many plants. While areas of shallow water at the edges will allow you to grow interesting marsh plants, be sure that at least two-thirds of the surface area has 600 mm of water below it. This will enable you to grow deep-water plants such as water lilies and lotus and it will also

Two pools have been used to achieve this water garden. Water from the upper pool gurgles over rocks into a second pool 300 mm below. The upper pool is above ground but looks natural surrounded by rocks and foliage.

help protect fish from cats, birds and sunburn.

BUILDING THE POND

Begin by laying out the plan. For an irregular, natural looking pond, establish the shoreline with a long piece of rope or garden hose. If you want a square or rectangular pond, use a stringline stretched taut between stakes. Be realistic about the size of hole you can dig. If you try to create a lake and then can't finish the digging, you'll end up with an undesirable large, shallow area of water.

A pond liner is the easiest way to contain water. The best liners are

BUILDING A POND

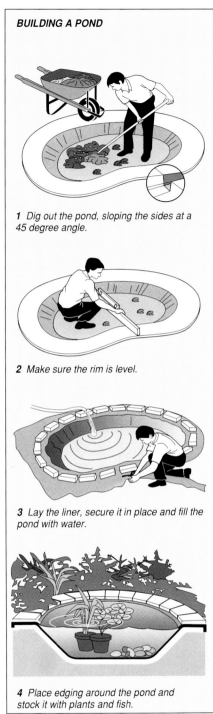

1 Dig out the pond, sloping the sides at a 45 degree angle.

2 Make sure the rim is level.

3 Lay the liner, secure it in place and fill the pond with water.

4 Place edging around the pond and stock it with plants and fish.

INSTALLING A CASCADE

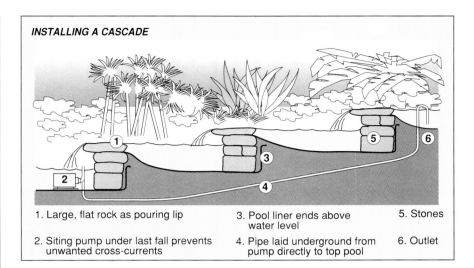

1. Large, flat rock as pouring lip
2. Siting pump under last fall prevents unwanted cross-currents
3. Pool liner ends above water level
4. Pipe laid underground from pump directly to top pool
5. Stones
6. Outlet

made from butyl rubber (or synthetic rubber). They are quite expensive but are guaranteed for twenty years and can be expected to last fifty. Black plastic is cheap but punctures easily and after a few years in the sun will have to be replaced. Or you can buy a readymade moulded fibreglass pond, although they restrict your choice of shape and size, or you can construct a pond from concrete. Unless it is expertly laid, however, concrete will soon crack and leak.

1 Start the excavation by scraping off the topsoil. This layer of dark, humusy soil is valuable and you should either spread it thinly over the rest of the garden or store it for later use. If you need to dispose of any soil, let it be the subsoil. Dig out the pond, sloping the sides at a 45 degree angle. If you like, around the edges you can incorporate shelves of shallow water for bog and marsh plants. Make provision for an overflow in the event of heavy rain and do consider where that water will go.

2 Use a level to make sure that the rim is even all round. Clear the edges and bottom of anything that could puncture the liner.

3 To lay the liner, first line the excavation with 50–80 mm of sand. Place the liner in the hole and mould it to the shape of the pond. It is not necessary to smooth out every wrinkle. Secure the edges of the liner with bricks and begin to fill it with water. As the pond fills, it may be necessary to release sections of the secured liner. After filling, let the pond lie for a week to settle in and to allow you to test for leaks.

4 To hide the overhanging liner, dig a trench 150 mm deep right around the pond. Lay the excess liner in the trench, trimming off any that can't be buried, and fill the trench with soil, sand or cement. Complete the pond by trimming the edge with rocks, bricks, sandstone or timber, making sure the trim hides the trench from sight.

CASCADES

Water flowing from a cascade will greatly increase the impact of your pond. A sloping garden is well suited to a cascade, but you can have an effective one on a flat block, too, as long as you keep the scheme low and wide so that it looks natural. Construct the waterway with liners, as for the pond. Stones can be placed at the edges of each fall for a more attractive appearance and to protect the lining from the constant force of the water. Each level of a stair-stepped cascade should have a vertical drop of at least 150 mm, although a fall of up to a metre can be very effective. But remember, the higher the lift, the smaller the volume of water a pump can handle. Flexible vinyl tubing can be used to transport water from the bottom to the top of the cascade.

A submersible pump pulls in water through a screen and then expels a steady stream of water through its outlet. To keep water moving gently, set the pump 50–100 mm above the pool bottom and then connect it safely to a source of electricity.

GLOSSARY

anchor bracket connector securing one part of a structure to another to make the parts stable

angle iron iron or steel bar with an L-shaped cross-section

baluster small post used to support a handrail

bearer sub-floor timber that supports floor joists

bevel sloping surface cut at an angle other than 90°

bird's mouth notch cut in a rafter so that it fits over a wall plate or beam

bullet-head nail general purpose nail with short, cylindrical head

butt hinges the wings of the hinge are of equal size and are screwed to the ends of the movable part and the frame so that only the knuckle of the hinge projects

cantilever beam or slab with a projecting, unsupported end

caulk fill a joint to make it water-tight or airtight

chamfer small bevel or slope on the edge of a board or timber

cleat piece of wood fastened onto something to give support

clout nail with a flat, circular head, usually galvanised

coach screw screw with a square or hexagonal head that can be turned with a spanner

compressed cement thick, dense version of fibro cement sheeting, used in places susceptible to damp

cuphead bolt large round-headed bolt, square under the head to prevent it turning

cupping (of boards) bending across the width of a board as the result of shrinkage

darby float wooden float or trowel about 1 m long

expansion strip soft material used to fill the joint between two surfaces to allow for expansion and contraction

finial decorative capping for a post

going width of the tread of a step, from one riser to the next

half-lap joint timber joint made by cutting recesses into both components to a depth of half the thickness of the timber, and overlapping the timbers

header brick laid with its length across the wall

housed joint T-joint where the end of one timber is fitted into a groove or housing in the other

jig device to hold a component during machining

joint strike trowel used to finish a mortar joint so that it slopes slightly upwards or downwards

joist beam supporting floorboards or ceiling

joist hanger U-shaped metal anchor that is attached to the bearer; the end of the joist fits into it

lath thin, narrow strip of wood

ledger horizontal timber fastened to a wall to support rafters of a pergola or other construction

masonry bolt bolt with a metal or plastic sleeve that expands to grip the masonry around a hole that is pre-drilled

nogging short, horizontal timber between wall studs

pergola angle connector suitable for outdoor use and used to fix together two members

post cap U-shaped metal stirrup that fits on top of a post to hold the beam

post support metal stirrup into which the base of a post fits, with a projection at the base that is embedded in cement

quad moulding in the shape of a quadrant of a circle

rebate step-shaped cut along the edge or face of a timber

ridge highest part of a roof where the upper ends of the rafters meet

riser the vertical face of a step

router power tool used to cut rebates (grooves) accurately and quickly

run (stair) going or width of a step; the total run is the horizontal distance between the top and bottom of a flight of steps

scarf joint joining of two pieces of timber together in length by cutting the ends so that they overlap and fit together

sill horizontal member at the bottom of a window frame

skew nail fasten with a nail at an oblique or slanting angle

span horizontal distance between the supports of a roof, floor, beam etc.

spreaders device for keeping apart and spacing parallel objects

stirrup (metal) U-shaped support

strap clamp device for securing objects together by means of a strap

stringer (stair) beam running diagonally up each side of a flight of stairs, supporting the steps

tread the part of a step that is trodden on

triple grip metal connector with three surfaces, used to fix together three members or surfaces

INDEX

Illustrative photographs are indicated in *italics*.

Published by Murdoch Books®,
a division of Murdoch Magazines Pty Limited, 213 Miller Street, North Sydney NSW 2060

Designer: Wing Ping Tong
Project Editor: Christine Eslick
Contributing Project Designers: Tony Fragar, Greg Cheetham, James R. Downing
Illustrations: Lorenzo Lucia
Photographs: Better Homes and Gardens®
Picture Library, Gale Australia Pty Ltd (pp. 18, 20 lower left),
Stirling Macoboy (p. 52), Geoffrey Burnie (p. 16)
and Peter Scott (pp. 34, 70, 76 top, 102 top)

Publisher: Anne Wilson
Publishing Manager: Mark Newman
Managing Editor: Susan Tomnay
Art Director: Lena Lowe
Production Manager: Catie Ziller
Marketing Manager: Mark Smith
National Sales Manager: Keith Watson
Picture Librarian: Dianne Bedford

National Library of Australia
Cataloguing-in-Publication Data
Outdoor structures.
Includes index.
ISBN 0 86411 318 8.
1. Garden structures - Design and construction - Amateurs' manuals.
690.89

© Copyright text, design, photography and illustrations Murdoch Books® 1994. All rights reserved. No part
of this publication may be reproduced, stored in a retrieval system or transmitted in any form or by any
means, electronic, mechanical, photocopying, recording or otherwise without the prior written permission of
the publisher. Murdoch Books® is a trade mark of Murdoch Magazines Pty Limited. Australian distribution
to supermarkets and newsagents by Gordon & Gotch Ltd, 68 Kingsgrove Road, Belmore NSW 2192
*Better Homes and Gardens® (Trade Mark) Regd T.M. of Meredith Corporation

Thanks to Reverend Milton Brown (The Forest Kirk, Frenchs Forest), the Fletcher family
and the Myors family for assistance with photography.